The Frank Dunlop Young Vic Production of

scapino!

a long way off from Molière
by Frank Dunlop and Jim Dale

D1440876

THE YOUNG VIC

THE DRAMATIC PUBLISHING COMPANY

SCAPINO!

For Ten Men and Four Women

CHARACTERS

OTTAVIO . . . *son of the wealthy merchant, Argante*
SYLVESTRO . . . . *Ottavio's guardian*
SCAPINO . . *friend of Sylvestro, Leandro's guardian*
GIACINTA . . . . *in love with Ottavio*
ARGANTE . . . . *father of Ottavio*
GERONTE . . . . *father of Leandro*
LEANDRO . . . . *friend of Ottavio, son of Geronte*
CARLO . . . . *a bum*
ZERBINETTA . . . . *a gypsy*
NURSE . . . . *of Giacinta*
HEADWAITER
TWO HARASSED WAITERS (One singing)
ONE WAITRESS (Lives in cafe)

TIME: *The present.*

PLACE: *The seaport of Naples, a cafe bar at the side of the dock.*

What People Are Saying...

"Excellent—a crowd pleaser. The material was both challenging and understandable for high school kids. We had a blast and ended up with a very tight production."

Shon Denby,
DeKalb School of the Arts,
Atlanta, Ga.

"The first act can be slow but the second act is hilarious. The scene where Geronte hides in a sack while Scapino pretends to be pirates, soldiers, etc., is laugh-out-loud funny. I'm not a big fan of audience participation, but here it was great fun!"

Norman McPhee,
Racine Theater Guild,
Racine, Wis.

"Excellent play for high schools. It allows for lots of creativity on part of director and cast. It is fast moving and funny."

Stan Strickler,
Stark County High School,
Toulon, Ill.

part one

No house curtain is used. The stage is preset (see Production Notes, pages 87-88) and the curtain opened fifteen minutes before the show begins.

(WAITRESS enters from cafe, yawning; puts five coins in jukebox, and selects songs. Jukebox does not begin so she kicks and slaps it. Music begins on slap. WAITRESS does warm-up exercises to music and exits into cafe. CARLO enters theatre from stage L and talks to audience in mock Italian. He climbs over barrels and boxes at LC and starts to cross R. WAITRESS enters cafe balcony and picks up three tablecloths (L to R) from railing. CARLO is C as he and WAITRESS on balcony exchange nasty glances. Seagulls are heard. WAITRESS exits as CARLO enters audience from stairs at stage RC, talking to audience in mock Italian. Guitar solo of song "Minestrone Macaroni" is heard from inside cafe. Three WAITERS enter from cafe, jukebox stops, first hummed measures of "Minestrone Macaroni" is heard. HEADWAITER supervises setting up of cafe from UC. WAITER 1 crosses to R table, places broom against table, crosses to DC table and sets chairs. WAITER 2 crosses to L table, sets chairs and sweeps area in front of cafe. SCAPINO enters cafe balcony playing second measure of "Minestrone Macaroni." Seagulls

fade. WAITRESS enters with tablecloths from
cafe. She crosses to L table and leaves tablecloth. SCAPINO on cafe balcony and backstage
singers begin singing "Minestrone Macaroni. "
They continue singing during the ensuing
action.

MINESTRONE MACARONI

Pollo All Americana,
Scampi Fritti in Brodo
Pasta Bolognese,
Pate Mayonnaise,
Capuchino Espresso

Minestrone Macaroni,
Ravioli Aux Crevette,
Caramella In Padella,
Avocado Vinaigrette.

Scallopina Valdostana
Bistecca Con Risotto,
Pasta Bolognese
Pate Mayonnaise
Da Un Buon Appetito.

Minestrone Macaroni,
Ravioli Aux Crevette,
Caramella In Padella,
Avocado Vinaigrette.

WAITRESS crosses to R table and leaves tablecloth. WAITER 1 finishes setting chairs at
downstage table. He starts to get broom, sees
CARLO entering from R and chases him into
audience, yelling in mock Italian. WAITRESS
shakes out third tablecloth, crosses to downstage

table as WAITER 1 crosses to table R, passing
her on bridge. He fixes chairs and begins
sweeping stage R area. WAITRESS places
tablecloth on downstage table. CARLO enters
stage, sits at downstage table in right chair and
pinches her bottom. At first she doesn't react,
then as he persists she slaps him and begins to
cross upstage. CARLO pulls tablecloth over him
like a blanket and goes to sleep. WAITRESS sees
him, screams at him in mock Italian, grabs
tablecloth, pulls him out of chair and throws
him down stairs. He yells at her in mock
Italian and then begins talking to audience.
WAITRESS fixes tablecloth at table, crosses
to R table and, with back to audience, fixes
tablecloth. CARLO sneaks up behind her, looks
up her skirt, looks to audience and looks up her
skirt again. WAITRESS starts to cross to L.
CARLO climbs on mainstage and exits R.
WAITER 1 throws broom to HEADWAITER, goes
down on knee and makes a pass at WAITRESS
as she pushes him out of her way. At this
point, lyrics end, and melody of "Minestrone
Macaroni" is hummed.

HEADWAITER throws his broom to WAITER 2
and makes a pass at WAITRESS as she pushes
him out of the way. As WAITRESS crosses toward
table L, WAITER 2 throws both brooms to
HEADWAITER and falls on his knee and makes
pass at WAITRESS. She slaps his face, straightens
tablecloth, and exits L. HEADWAITER throws
both brooms to WAITER 1 and all WAITERS cross
to exit into cafe. HEADWAITER exits through
cafe doors, and bicycle horn is heard off R.
WAITER 1 and WAITER 2 see CARLO approaching
cafe from R on a bicycle. They run to cafe and

open doors as CARLO rides through doors and
into cafe, followed by the WAITERS. A loud
crash is heard from inside cafe followed by much
hubbub and confusion.

CARLO is thrown out of cafe by the seat of his
pants and back of his neck by WAITER 1.
WAITER 1 re-enters cafe as WAITER 2 exits
cafe and throws a bicycle wheel at CARLO.
WAITER 2 enters cafe as WAITER 1 exits cafe
and throws handlebars at CARLO. WAITER 1
enters cafe as WAITER 2 exits cafe and throws
bicycle seat at CARLO. WAITER 2 enters cafe
as WAITER 1 throws SYLVESTRO out of cafe,
who then falls on his knees next to CARLO.
CARLO whispers to SYLVESTRO as WAITER 1
enters cafe. SYLVESTRO stands and runs DR
to meet OTTAVIO, who has entered from the R
aisle and is mounting the steps to the forestage.
SYLVESTRO grabs him and says, "Your father
is back." Meanwhile CARLO has picked up the
three bicycle parts and exits R. Yelling an
Italian expletive, OTTAVIO runs on stage to
in front of bench at C, and turns.)

OTTAVIO. I'm lost, I'm ruined, what am I to do?
     Sad news to an enamored heart! My world is
     crumbling around me. Disaster after disaster.
     You've just heard, Sylvestro, that my father is
     back.
SYLVESTRO. Your father is back.
OTTAVIO. His boat docked this very morning.
SYLVESTRO (sitting at downstage table, in right
     chair). This very morning.
OTTAVIO (moving a bit toward R). And that he's
     come back determined to marry me off.
SYLVESTRO. To marry you off.

OTTAVIO. To a daughter of Signor Geronte.

SYLVESTRO. Of Signor Geronte.

OTTAVIO (down to bridge). And the daughter is
    already on her way back from Marseilles to do
    the deed.

SYLVESTRO. To do the deed.

OTTAVIO. And this news was sent by my uncle.

SYLVESTRO. By your uncle.

OTTAVIO (crossing below SYLVESTRO toward left
    chair). To whom my father sent it in a letter.

SYLVESTRO. In a letter.

OTTAVIO. And my uncle knows all we've been up to.

SYLVESTRO. All we've been up to.

OTTAVIO (placing hat on table and sitting). Oh, for
    heaven's sake, say something instead of parroting
    everything I say. (Hits table.)

SYLVESTRO. Parroting every -- (Hits hat instead
    of table.) -- what more can I say? (Fixing hat.)
    You've remembered everything, spot on.

OTTAVIO. Well, at least give me some advice.
    Tell me how I can get out of this terrible mess.

SYLVESTRO (an Italian expletive: "Oi Mama Leone").
    I'm just as much in the mess as you are. I could
    do with a bit of advice myself.

OTTAVIO. I'm ruined by this rotten return.

SYLVESTRO. The ruin's mutual.

OTTAVIO (standing and moving R). When my father
    finds out, I can see a thunderstorm of violent
    recriminations pouring on me. (SCAPINO exits
    cafe balcony.)

SYLVESTRO. Recriminations pouring are nothing.
    It's me what'll have to suffer most. I can see a
    thunderstorm of belts on the ear bursting on me.

OTTAVIO. Oh, God, how can I get out of this terrible
    mess!

SYLVESTRO. You should have thought of that before
    you got into it.

OTTAVIO (crossing bridge). It's not the time now to
    say "I told you so." What can I do? (Now he
    jumps across the water to SYLVESTRO.)
SYLVESTRO. I don't know.
OTTAVIO. What can I do? What can I do? (Grabs
    SYLVESTRO by neck and nearly pushes him
    into sea.)
SYLVESTRO. I can't swim.

(Enter SCAPINO from cafe.)

SCAPINO. How now, Signor Ottavio?
SYLVESTRO (pulling away from OTTAVIO). Scapino!
SCAPINO (crossing toward bridge). Hey! Hey!
    What's the matter? What's wrong with you?
    Something seems to be wrong . . . you look a
    little disturbed.
OTTAVIO (crossing bridge). Oh, my dear Scapino,
    I'm ruined. I'm going mad. I'm the unhappiest
    man in the whole world.
SCAPINO. Really? How's that?
OTTAVIO. You mean to say you haven't heard what's
    happened to me?
SCAPINO. No.
OTTAVIO (grabbing him by sleeve). My father and
    Signor Geronte are back, and they're determined
    to marry me off.
SCAPINO. Well, what's so horrible in that?
OTTAVIO (clutching sleeve). Oh, if only you knew
    the cause of my trouble.
SCAPINO. There, there, just you tell me everything.
    You know I'm always willing to listen when a
    young fellow's in trouble.
OTTAVIO (pulling SCAPINO downstage). Oh,
    Scapino, if you can devise any means to get me
    out of this terrible mess that I'm in -- (Kneeling.)
    -- I'll be indebted to you for the rest of my life.

SCAPINO. Well, there's not much I can't do once
I've set my mind on it. The good Lord has
blessed me with quite a genius for clever ideas
and inspired inventions, which the less talented,
in their jealousies, call deceits and trickery.
(Moves toward SYLVESTRO.) But without a
shadow of a doubt, there's never been another
fellow to measure up to me -- (Lifting chocolate
bar from SYLVESTRO's pocket.) -- when it
comes down to a little bit of fiddling or making
a slight adjustment in a tight situation. Chocolate?
(Offering chocolate to SYLVESTRO and then,
going DC, to audience.) There's no one with a
better reputation at the job, but talent and hard
work just aren't appreciated these days. (Goes
up to chair earlier vacated by OTTAVIO.) Since
my affairs got a little troubled, I've given the
whole thing up.

OTTAVIO (on the bridge). What affairs and what
troubles, Scapino?

SCAPINO. Oh, I had a little contretemps with the
law.

OTTAVIO. With the law?

SCAPINO (sitting). Yes, we didn't quite agree on a
certain matter.

SYLVESTRO. They didn't quite agree. (Sits.)

SCAPINO. You know they treated me very badly, and
I was so struck by the ingratitude of my fellow
men I decided I would never lift up another finger
from that day on to help anybody. But I'm
always willing to listen.

OTTAVIO. You know, Scapino, that two months
ago Signor Geronte and my father set sail
together on a business trip in which both their
interests were concerned.

SCAPINO. Quite.

OTTAVIO (moving toward table). And that Leandro

and myself were left by our fathers, myself in
the care of Sylvestro -- (Hitting SYLVESTRO on
the back.) — and Leandro under your supervision.
SCAPINO. And I've done my job very conscientiously.
SYLVESTRO (standing). So have I. . . .
OTTAVIO (pushing SYLVESTRO back into chair).
   Some time afterwards Leandro met a young
   gypsy girl and fell madly in love with her.
SCAPINO (laughing). Quite.
OTTAVIO (going back across the bridge). As we're
   great friends he took me straight away into his
   confidence and we went together to see the girl.
   Well, I thought she was quite pretty, but not as
   pretty as he thought I would. He spoke about
   nothing but her, day in, day out; hardly a moment
   went by that he didn't boast to me about her
   beauty, her charm, her wit, her every word.
   In fact, he got quite annoyed with me because I
   wasn't as lovesick as he was.
SCAPINO. Look . . . look . . . look . . . I don't
   quite see where all this is leading up to.
OTTAVIO (after a slight pause). One day . . .
SCAPINO. Ah!
OTTAVIO. When I was going with him to visit his
   obsession, we heard in a little house on a by-
   street, the sound of sobbing mixed with a great
   many tears. We asked what was going on.
SCAPINO. Yes, well, you would, wouldn't you?
   (To audience.) You'd say "What was going on?"
   Wouldn't you?
OTTAVIO. A woman passing by told us two foreign
   women lived there in terrible conditions.
SCAPINO. Well, what next?
OTTAVIO (mimes dragging LEANDRO). Curiosity
   made me drag Leandro to see what was the
   matter. (Goes to bench as he mimes entering
   room.) We went into a little room where we saw

an old woman dying . . . (SCAPINO and
SYLVESTRO "Ah.") . . . a nurse crying . . .
(SCAPINO and SYLVESTRO "Ah.") . . . and a
young girl dissolved in tears, the most beautiful,
the most exquisite that was ever seen.

SCAPINO. Ah-ha. Oi-oi.

OTTAVIO. Any other girl would have looked wretched
in the state she was, wearing nothing . . .

SCAPINO and SYLVESTRO (double take). Eh . . .

OTTAVIO. . . . but rags, hair falling disheveled
about her shoulders, but even in that state she
glittered like a thousand stars. (SYLVESTRO
gets up, starts across the bridge.)

SCAPINO. Yes, I'm beginning to get the point,
yessssss. . . .

OTTAVIO. If you'd seen her, Scapino, in the state
I had found her, you would have found her
devastating.

SCAPINO. I don't doubt it. And without seeing her
I realize she must have that certain . . .
(SYLVESTRO and SCAPINO: "Whoops.") . . .
something. (SYLVESTRO has now crossed L
and disappeared into the cafe.)

OTTAVIO. Her tears weren't those ugly tears which
make a face red and swollen. (Moves a few
steps toward R.) She cried in the prettiest way
imaginable, and her misery was the most
beautiful misery in the world.

SCAPINO. Yes. . . . Obviously.

(SYLVESTRO comes from the cafe with two Cokes
and glasses and returns to the table as OTTAVIO
continues.)

OTTAVIO. Sobbing . . . (Kneels.) . . . she threw
herself on her knees beside the dying woman, and
called her "Mother."

RO. Eh. (Stopping momentarily by
AVIO.)

IO. Everyone felt tears come into their eyes
see such love and affection. (SYLVESTRO, now
at table, turns bottles over into glasses.)

SCAPINO. Very moving indeed, and I suppose that
one lot of love and affection sort of gave birth to
another.

OTTAVIO. Scapino, a stone wall would have loved
her.

SCAPINO. Quite.

(SYLVESTRO, realizing the Coke bottles are
unopened, runs and hands them to OTTAVIO
and runs back to SCAPINO. In frustration,
OTTAVIO tries to take bottle top off with his
teeth and then with his shoe. He then uses
Coke bottles as binoculars. He looks to cafe
and slowly turns R, looking through "binoculars."
CARLO enters from R, walks to OTTAVIO,
observing the activity, and stops in front of
him as OTTAVIO sees CARLO through "binoculars." CARLO takes bottle opener from
pocket, shows it to OTTAVIO, who gives him
one of the bottles. CARLO opens the bottle,
puts top in OTTAVIO's hand /OTTAVIO is
listening to SYLVESTRO/ and begins exit
toward cafe. OTTAVIO extends his bottle for
a toast, CARLO stops, clinks bottles and exits
through cafe drinking Coke. OTTAVIO tries to
drink his Coke and realizes the cap is still on.)

SYLVESTRO. Now look, if you don't cut the story
short we'll be listening here till tomorrow. Now
I'll finish it in two words. His heart burst into
flames. He couldn't live without the girl. He's
never off the doorstep. His visits to comfort the

unhappy girl make him more of a lodger than a
visitor. The nurse forbids him the house.
Irresistible force. (SYLVESTRO and
SCAPINO: "Immovable object.") He begs, he
grovels, he argues. Not a hope. For though
the girl is without money and friends, she
comes from a good family, and unless he marries
her, he's got to keep his hands off her.
(SYLVESTRO moves R, then up across the bridge,
turning back again as he continues his speech.)
Passion feeds on obstacles. He wracks his brain,
ponders, reasons, debates and then makes up
his mind, and he's been a married man for the
last three days. Now add to that the unexpected
return of his father; add to that the other marriage
his father's arranged with Signor Geronte's
daughter, that's the daughter of a second wife
Geronte married at Marseilles. (OTTAVIO
comes beside SYLVESTRO, who is now standing
on the bridge.)

OTTAVIO (handing Coke back to SYLVESTRO). And
worse than all this, add the poverty in which my
poor, lovely wife now lives and my inability,
penniless as I am, to help her. (Sits on rope.)

SYLVESTRO. There.

SCAPINO (standing, crossing to OTTAVIO). Is that
all? Do you know the pair of you seem bowled
over by nothing. I mean, what on earth are you
worried for? (Goes up on bridge.) Aren't you
ashamed to be panicked by such a little thing?
What the devil, you've been to the Actor's Studio,
and you can't stir your brain to some little
stratagem, some little wheeze to put things
right. (Now in front of bench.) Do you know
I was no bigger than that, when I was clearing
up matters a thousand times more complicated.
Oh, if only my legal mix-up had not made me

swear off such temptation.

SYLVESTRO (moving to right end of bench as
        SCAPINO moves to left end).   Yes, well, I
        realize I haven't been blessed with your brains.

SCAPINO.   That's true, very true.

SYLVESTRO.   And that I haven't got your genius . . .

(GIAOINTA enters top of R aisle.)

SYLVESTRO.   . . . for getting mixed up with the
        law, but . . .

GIACINTA (seeing OTTAVIO and running toward
        him).   Ottavio!

OTTAVIO (going to her).   Here comes my lovely
        Giacinta.

GIACINTA.   Ottavio! (They meet at the lower end
        of the bridge. GIACINTA kisses OTTAVIO and
        kneels. SCAPINO and SYLVESTRO sit on
        bench and watch.)   Oh, Ottavio, is it true what
        Sylvestro told Nerina? Your father's back and
        is going to marry you to someone else? (With
        tears in her eyes.)

OTTAVIO.   Yes, my dearest, and I'm as heartbroken
        as you are. But -- (Kneeling.) -- what's this?
        You're crying. Why these tears? Surely you
        don't suspect that I'll be unfaithful to you?
        Surely you don't doubt my love for you?

GIACINTA.   Yes, Ottavio, I'm sure you love me, but
        I'm not so sure you'll always love me.

OTTAVIO.   How could anyone love you without loving
        you for the rest of one's life?

GIACINTA (crossing to L).   I've heard, Ottavio, that
        your sex loves not so long as ours does, and
        those burning passions men discover are as
        easily extinguished as they are set alight. (Turns
        to OTTAVIO.)

OTTAVIO (rising).   My dear Giacinta, I'm not <u>made</u>

like other men . . .

SCAPINO and SYLVESTRO (crossing left legs over
    right). Oh, my God!

OTTAVIO (crossing to GIACINTA).   . . . I know that
    I shall love you till I die.

GIACINTA (crossing to original position at R). I'm
    sure you believe what you say, and I don't doubt
    that your words are sincere, but I fear a stronger
    adversary than the tender feelings you have for
    me. You're completely dependent on your father,
    who is determined to marry you to someone else.
    If that happens I expect I'll die. (She sits on
    bridge step and bursts into tears.)

OTTAVIO (crossing to her, kneeling, and taking her
    hands). No father shall make me break my word
    to you. (SCAPINO and SYLVESTRO cross to
    behind GIACINTA and OTTAVIO, joking as if
    they are on a film set shooting a love scene,
    SCAPINO miming camera and SYLVESTRO using
    Coke bottle as microphone. They return to
    bench. OTTAVIO and GIACINTA stand.) I would
    rather give up my country, life itself, than give
    up you. Already without having seen her I hate
    the girl he wishes me to marry. Don't cry,
    dearest Giacinta, your tears hurt me more than
    you, every one -- (Kisses her eye.) --wounds
    me -- (Kisses other eye.) -- to the heart.
    (Kisses her lips.)

GIACINTA (crossing again L). To make you happy,
    I shall hold back my tears, and wait with dry
    eyes for whatever Fate has in store.

OTTAVIO (crossing L to GIACINTA). Fate is on our
    side.

GIACINTA. It must be, if you stay true to me.

OTTAVIO. Never doubt that.

GIACINTA. Then I shall be happy. (They hug.)

SCAPINO (to SYLVESTRO). She's not such a fool --

eh! (Stands.) She's quite nice to look at, too.
(SCAPINO begins to exit R.) Ciao!

OTTAVIO (turning and running after SCAPINO).
Here's a man who could be a marvelous help to
us if he were willing.

SCAPINO (stopping and turning to OTTAVIO and
GIACINTA). Now, you know I've resolved never
to meddle in anyone else's business again -- no
. . . but . . . (Staring at GIACINTA.) . . . if
you were both to ask me very nicely . . .
perhaps . . .

OTTAVIO. Oh, if it's only a question of asking
nicely, my dearest Scapino -- (Going on his
knees.) I beg you with all my heart to be the
captain of our ship.

SCAPINO (still staring at GIACINTA, then turning
to OTTAVIO). Pardon . . . Ah, yes. (Crosses
down and pats OTTAVIO's head and says to
GIACINTA.) And you, have you nothing to say
to me? (SCAPINO wipes hand.)

GIACINTA (crossing to SCAPINO). I beg you by
everything that's dear to you to help us and our
love. (She grabs his tie, pulls him to her in
three moves and kisses him.)

SCAPINO (after kiss). Right, I've been argued
'round. You get along, then; I'll do some
thinking on your behalf. (GIACINTA starts to
exit DR. SYLVESTRO crosses UL to cafe and
puts Coke on barrel by cafe door.)

OTTAVIO. Believe me, I . . .

SCAPINO. Chut! (To GIACINTA.) Just get along
home and stop worrying. Ciao!

GIACINTA (exiting DR, turning at foot of stairs).
Ciao!

SCAPINO. Ciao!

GIACINTA (still exiting, crossing L below stage). Ciao!

SCAPINO (to SYLVESTRO). What a lovely girl. Ciao!

GIACINTA (exiting stage L aisle). Ciao! (SCAPINO
    throws her a kiss.)

SCAPINO (to OTTAVIO). Ah, yes . . . you get your
    upper lip stiffened to meet your father.

OTTAVIO (crossing to chair at R table, and sitting).
    I must admit my lip's trembling already. I suffer
    from a sort of natural cowardice that I just can't
    overcome.

SCAPINO. You must seem master from the moment
    you meet, or he'll take advantage of your weakness
    and treat you like a child. You must learn to look
    com — com — com — (To SYLVESTRO, who has
    crossed back to SCAPINO.) What's the word?
    . . . Com —

SYLVESTRO. . . . um . . . compost.

SCAPINO. Composed. A little boldness, and answer
    him firmly whatever he says.

(CARLO enters from cafe drinking glass of Coke.
    SYLVESTRO meets him at bench and takes Coke.
    CARLO takes Coke bottle from pocket and drinks.
    The others watch.)

OTTAVIO. I'll do the best I can. (He stands.)

SCAPINO. Right. We could have a little rehearsal
    here to get you used to it. We have the audience
    here. We'll play the scene together and see how
    well you'll act it. Now, don't forget. Mind
    resolute, head high, firm looks.

OTTAVIO (taking pose). Like this?

SCAPINO. Come on. . . . Firm looks, head high, chin out.

OTTAVIO. O. K. now?

SCAPINO (crossing DL). Yes, that's all right. Now
    imagine I'm your father just arrived and answer
    me firmly as if I were him. I'm coming on now.
    (Imitating ARGANTE.) "Who ever heard of such
    a thing? What an idiot thing to do. (CARLO and

SYLVESTRO choke on their Cokes and spit
them into sea.) Ah, there you are worthless,
notorious -- (Crossing R.) -- son, unworthy
of a father like me. How dare you stand before
me after this fine behavior, this cheap trick
you've played whilst I've been away. Is this
the fruit of all my toils, lout? (He has now
reached OTTAVIO.) The respect you owe me,
the respect you owe me for my care of you?"
Say something! (OTTAVIO tries to say something
but SCAPINO stops him.) "You have the cheek,
you beetle, to get married without your father's
consent -- to marry secretly without even his
knowledge? Answer me, you lout, answer me.
Give me one good reason." (OTTAVIO tries to
say something again with arm and forefinger
extended. He fails, his finger, then arm, slowly
collapsing.)

OTTAVIO. It's because you sound exactly like my
        father.
SCAPINO. Well, of course I do. That's why you
        mustn't act like an idiot.
OTTAVIO. I'll do better this time. I'll be firm
        and . . . (Gulp.) . . . determined.
SCAPINO. Determined?
OTTAVIO. Determined.
SCAPINO. Definitely?
OTTAVIO. Definitely.
SYLVESTRO. Good. Here comes your father now.

(ARGANTE growls from lobby, then runs down L
        house aisle to forestage.)

OTTAVIO. Oh, God, I'm lost. (He rushes off R.
        CARLO leaves through cafe and SYLVESTRO
        crosses in to cafe, coming out on balcony.)

SCAPINO. Hey there, Ottavio, hold on a minute.
    Quite a turn of speed! What a weak-kneed
    specimen. Well, Sylvestro, we'll have to deal
    with the old man ourselves.
SYLVESTRO (on balcony). What shall I tell him?
SCAPINO. Well . . . agree with me and back me
    up. (Exits cafe. ARGANTE, speaking to him-
    self, is now on forestage.)
ARGANTE. Who ever heard of such a thing. (Bangs
    table with cane and crosses to table R.)

(HEADWAITER enters, crosses to table and mimes
    taking order from ARGANTE.)

SYLVESTRO. He's already heard about it, and he's
    so furious that he's having a row with himself
    about it.
ARGANTE. What a lunatic thing to do. (Bangs table.)

(SCAPINO enters cafe balcony.)

SCAPINO. Let's listen awhile.
ARGANTE. I'd love to know what they dare to say
    to me about this damned marriage. (Bangs
    table. HEADWAITER checks off appetizer on
    menu.)
SCAPINO. We're just thinking about it.
ARGANTE. Will they try to deny it?
SCAPINO. No, I don't think we'll do that.
ARGANTE. Or will they try to make excuses?
SCAPINO. That's possible.
ARGANTE. Perhaps they'll try to entertain me with
    fairy stories. (Bangs table. HEADWAITER
    checks off entree.)
SCAPINO. Perhaps. Eh?
ARGANTE. Everything they say will be useless.
    (Bangs table. HEADWAITER checks off dessert

and exits to cafe.)

SCAPINO. We'll see about that.

ARGANTE. They shan't make an idiot of me.

SCAPINO. Ho ho. Don't you count on it.

ARGANTE. I'll make sure that rascal of a son of
mine is kept safe.

SCAPINO. And we've the same intention.

ARGANTE. And as for that ferret Sylvestro, I'll
. . . I'll . . . I'll . . . beat him to a jelly.

SYLVESTRO. I knew he'd remember me. (SCAPINO
and SYLVESTRO do hand-slapping game. Seeing
SYLVESTRO on balcony and SCAPINO leaving
balcony, ARGANTE runs to cafe.)

ARGANTE. Ah-ha. So you're there, are you?
(Jumps under balcony and hits balcony with
cane, causing SYLVESTRO to jump.) Wise
custodian of a family -- (ARGANTE hits balcony
and SYLVESTRO jumps.) -- fine director of
morals of the young. (ARGANTE hits balcony
and SYLVESTRO jumps.)

(SCAPINO enters from cafe and takes ARGANTE by
the arm, drawing him toward C stage.)

SCAPINO. Sir, I am ravished to see you home again.

ARGANTE. How do, Scapino. (Breaks away from
SCAPINO and goes back to under balcony. To
SYLVESTRO.) You've carried out my orders
very prettily, haven't you? (Hits balcony and
SYLVESTRO jumps.)

SYLVESTRO. I've done my best.

ARGANTE. My son's behaved himself only too well
whilst I've been away. (Hits balcony and
SYLVESTRO jumps.)

SCAPINO (taking ARGANTE by the arm again).
You're looking very well as far as I can see.

ARGANTE. Glowing. (Breaking away from SCAPINO

and saying to SYLVESTRO.) Well, can't you
say anything, idiot? (Hits balcony and
SYLVESTRO jumps.) Can't you say anything?
(Hits balcony and SYLVESTRO jumps.)
SCAPINO (taking ARGANTE by arm again and
crossing to R). Did you have a pleasant journey
back, sir? (SYLVESTRO exits balcony.)
ARGANTE (breaking away from SCAPINO as they
near the bench at C). Very pleasant, and for
God's sake, leave me alone and let me have a
row in peace.
SCAPINO (following, as ARGANTE continues R).
You want a row?
ARGANTE. Yes, I want a row.
SCAPINO. With whom, sir?

(SYLVESTRO enters from cafe. ARGANTE points to
him with his cane.)

ARGANTE. With that streak there. (During the
ensuing dialogue, SYLVESTRO unobtrusively
moves to sit on the bridge by going down the steps
L, by the boat, then down again, and crossing
below forestage to R and up onto the bridge with-
out using the steps. He listens to the conversation.)
SCAPINO. And why?
ARGANTE. You've not heard what's gone on whilst
I've been away?
SCAPINO. Well . . . well . . . I did hear a few
little jokey things, sir.
ARGANTE (crossing to table on forestage). A few
little jokey things! A catastrophe like this?
SCAPINO (following to bridge). Maybe you see things
a little differently.
ARGANTE. An astounding piece of insolence like this.
SCAPINO. Weeeeeeeellllllllll . . .
ARGANTE (sitting at table). A son to get married

without the consent of his father.

(WAITER 1 enters, crosses to table on forestage
    and places napkin, spoon and fork.)

SCAPINO. Yes, I know, it is very unusual. But I
    don't think you should make too much fuss about
    it.
ARGANTE. Well, I do think I should. (WAITER 1
    finishes setting table and exits.) And I'll have
    my bellyful of making a fuss about it. Don't
    you think I've got every reason in the world to
    be furious?

(HEADWAITER enters from cafe, crosses to C stage
    and checks off dishes on order pad as they are
    brought on and handed to SCAPINO, who places
    them in front of ARGANTE.)

SCAPINO. Quite. (Puts napkin around ARGANTE.)

(CARLO enters house and makes his way to stage.)

SCAPINO. I was just the same myself, sir, just
    after I heard the news.

(WAITER 2 enters with bread and crosses to
    SCAPINO.)

SCAPINO. . . . and I was so incensed on your
    behalf I had an enormous row with your son.

(WAITER 1 enters carrying spaghetti.)

SCAPINO. You just ask him how I shouted . . .

(SCAPINO takes bread from WAITER 2, who crosses

to take wine from WAITRESS /who enters from
cafe/ to give to SCAPINO.)

SCAPINO.   . . . how I lectured to him on the respect
he owed a father whose footsteps he's not good
enough to kiss. (CARLO, on stage, prepares to
shine ARGANTE's shoes.) You couldn't have
done better yourself, sir, but what good does
it do? I sat down and I thought and I reasoned
-- (Taking wine.) --out that at the bottom of it
all he might not be so much in the wrong as one
might think.   (All WAITERS and WAITRESS exit.
CARLO puts ARGANTE's foot on shoebox.
SCAPINO sits and pours wine.)

ARGANTE (pulling foot away from CARLO). What
kind of clever double-talk is this? There's
nothing wrong in getting married --point-blank --
to a stranger?

SCAPINO. Yes, but . . . what would you have him
do? Fate led him to it. (CARLO takes
ARGANTE's foot again and shines his shoe.
SCAPINO hands ARGANTE a glass of wine and
takes one for himself.)

ARGANTE. Oh-ho, the easiest excuse in the world.
One's only to commit the worst crimes
imaginable, cheat, steal, murder and say for
excuse, "Fate led me to it." (SCAPINO begins
readying spaghetti on fork.)

SCAPINO. Oh, good Lord, sir, no . . . no . . . no.
. . . You take my words too literally. No, I
meant to say that he found himself fatally
embroiled in this affair.

ARGANTE. Why . . . (SCAPINO puts forkful of
spaghetti in ARGANTE's mouth. Audience
laughs. CARLO spits in shoeshine rag.
ARGANTE reacts with a mouthful of spaghetti.)
Why did he become fatally embroiled?

SCAPINO (readying more spaghetti). Now surely, sir, you can't expect him to have the intelligence that you have? Young folks are . . .

ARGANTE. Young . . . (More spaghetti in ARGANTE's mouth.)

SCAPINO (breaking off a piece of roll). Exactly. And haven't the intelligence to keep them on the straight and narrow, doing nothing but what's reasonable. Now take our Leandro, for example . . .

ARGANTE (having chewed spaghetti). Oh! . . .

SCAPINO (putting bread in ARGANTE's mouth). . . . in spite of all I've taught him, in spite of all my remonstrances, has gone and done worse than your son.

ARGANTE. Worse than my son?

SCAPINO (nodding his head). Yes!

ARGANTE. He has? Tell me more. (CARLO stops shining shoes and listens.)

SCAPINO. Now, weren't you young once yourself, and didn't you once sow the odd wild oat? I've heard that you were quite a one for the signorinas in your day, and when you made an attack you never withdrew till the defenses were down.

ARGANTE (laughing, with mouthful of food). Yes, that's true. I don't know who the devil told you, but it's very true.

ARGANTE and SCAPINO (to each other). It's very true. (To the audience.) It's very true. (To the audience with CARLO.) It's very true.

ARGANTE. You've made a point there. But I never got myself into the fix he's done.

SCAPINO (standing). What would you have him do? He sees a young lady who shows an affection for him, for he takes after you to have all the women in love with him. (CARLO getting chummy with ARGANTE.)

ARGANTE. Yes, yes, yes, I know.

SCAPINO (moving to bridge). He finds her enchanting.
    He pays her visits, murmurs sweet nothings, sighs
    with passion. She lets herself be caught, he
    pushes his luck. Whoops! Surprised with her
    by her parents he's manhandled to the church
    where he is forced at gunpoint to marry her.

SYLVESTRO (standing). How does he do it?

SCAPINO (to ARGANTE, moving back to table). Look,
    would you have had him let himself be killed, sir?
    It's a far, far better thing to be married than to
    be dead. (CARLO stands up, claps and says
    "Bravo.")

ARGANTE (standing). They didn't tell me it had
    happened quite like that.

SCAPINO. Well, just you ask him, sir. He'll give
    you the same answer. (ARGANTE crosses to
    SYLVESTRO. CARLO sits in ARGANTE's chair
    and eats crumbs from bread basket.)

ARGANTE. Was it by force that he was married?

SYLVESTRO. No -- yes, signor.

SCAPINO (who has followed ARGANTE). Would I
    tell you a lie, sir?

ARGANTE. Well, then he should have gone straight
    to the police and reported the assault.

SCAPINO. That's just what he couldn't do.

ARGANTE. It would have made it much easier for me
    to dissolve the marriage.

SCAPINO. Dissolve the marriage?

ARGANTE. Yes.

SCAPINO. You wouldn't dissolve it.

ARGANTE. I wouldn't dissolve it?

SCAPINO. No!

ARGANTE. No?

SCAPINO. No!

ARGANTE. No?

SCAPINO. No!

ARGANTE. No?

SYLVESTRO. No! (Runs away, over the bridge to
    stage R.)

ARGANTE. What? (Crossing upstage.) Why shouldn'
    I have the rights of a father? And have satis-
    faction for the violence they've used against my
    son?

SCAPINO (following him upstage, then going to bench).
    It's something he won't really agree with.

ARGANTE. He won't really agree with?

SCAPINO. No.

ARGANTE. My son? (Goes to SCAPINO.)

SCAPINO (face to face with ARGANTE). Your son!
    Do you want him to have to confess publicly that
    he was frightened to death and that he was such a
    coward as to let himself be forced to marry her?
    He'd never be able to look anyone else in the face
    again. He'd feel himself unworthy of a father
    like you.

ARGANTE. That's a joke.

SCAPINO. No, look, he must for his honor and yours
    let everyone think he married her of his own free
    will.

ARGANTE (nose to nose with SCAPINO as text goes
    faster). And I must, for my honor and for his,
    prove the contrary.

SCAPINO. No. I don't think he'll do it.

ARGANTE. I'll force him to.

SCAPINO. He won't do it, I'm certain of it.

ARGANTE. He will do it, or I'll disinherit him.

SCAPINO. You?

ARGANTE. Me.

SCAPINO. Good.

ARGANTE. What do you mean, good?

SCAPINO. You won't disinherit him.

ARGANTE. I won't disinherit him?

SCAPINO. No.

ARGANTE. No?

SCAPINO. No.

ARGANTE. Very funny. I won't disinherit my son.

SCAPINO. No.

ARGANTE. And who is going to stop me?

SCAPINO. You will.

ARGANTE. Me?

SCAPINO. Yes, you. You won't have the heart to do it.

ARGANTE. I will.

SCAPINO. You're joking.

ARGANTE. I am not joking.

SCAPINO. Fatherly tenderness will prevail.

ARGANTE. Oh, no, it won't.

SCAPINO. Oh, yes, it will.

ARGANTE. I tell you, it shall be done.

SCAPINO (imitating ARGANTE). Oh . . . fff . . . fiddle-de-dee.

ARGANTE. Don't say "ff . . . fiddle-de-dee" to me.

SCAPINO. Now come on, sir, you're naturally too good-natured.

ARGANTE. I am not good-natured, not at all good-natured.

SYLVESTRO (crossing downstage, to audience). . . . He's not good-natured, not at all good-natured.

ARGANTE. . . . and I can be the very devil when I want to be. (Moves R.)

SCAPINO (crossing L, to audience). . . . oh, he is, too. Second act, he's fantastic.

ARGANTE. Let's have no more of this silly chitchat or I'll burst. (To SYLVESTRO.) Get out, pear-shape. Go and find that rascal of a son of mine whilst I go join Signor Geronte to tell him of the scandal. (SYLVESTRO runs down the steps and out.)

SCAPINO (returning to C). Sir, if I can be of any help

at any time, just you send for me. Call, and I
shall be at your service.

ARGANTE. Thank you. (To himself.) Oh, why
should Ottavio be an only child? If only my
daughter had been spared to me I'd have left
all my money to her. (Exits R. CARLO puts
away brush, rag and polish and runs after
ARGANTE.)

CARLO. Momento, Signore . . . Signore, momento.
(Stops near SCAPINO, who has come R.) . . .
shoeshine, signore?

SCAPINO. Suede, you're joking. (CARLO exits R.)

(SYLVESTRO, meanwhile, has mounted the steps to
the forestage and crossed R to SCAPINO.
HEADWAITER enters with bill on plate and
crosses to SCAPINO.)

SYLVESTRO. I agree, you're a genius, and you've
done marvelously well so far, but there's the
matter of money.

SCAPINO (taking plate from HEADWAITER). Money?
(Gives plate to SYLVESTRO and crosses to downstage table, pours wine and sits. SYLVESTRO puts
lire on plate and gives it to HEADWAITER.)

SYLVESTRO (crossing to downstage table and sitting).
Money. There's not only eating to consider, but
the creditors are beginning to chase me down the
street. (HEADWAITER takes lire, puts change
on plate and crosses to table.)

SCAPINO. Leave it to me. The plot is hatched.
(HEADWAITER at table offers change.
SYLVESTRO takes it and begins to put it in
his pocket. SCAPINO snaps his fingers, takes
coin and puts it on the plate as a tip.
SYLVESTRO takes it again. HEADWAITER
exits.) At the moment I am trying to think of a

man who I can trust to play a part I need.
(SCAPINO looks through audience, then to
SYLVESTRO who has been winding spaghetti
on his fork. SCAPINO grabs fork.) Hold it.
Make your hand into a fist. (SYLVESTRO does
it.) Put your hat on one side of your head.
(SYLVESTRO does so.) Stand up! (He does,
and so does SCAPINO.) Lean on one leg. (He
does.) Put that hand into your pocket. (He
does.) Now make your eyes into slits. (He
does.) Good! That's it. Can you see?

SYLVESTRO. No.

SCAPINO. Now strut around like one of those
gangsters in the films we've been watching.

SYLVESTRO (strutting around). Like this?

SCAPINO. I think we've been watching the wrong
films. Come on. Like this! Oh, yes, yes.
Now a couple-a more disguises for your face
and voice.

SYLVESTRO. Just as long as you don't get mixed up
with the law.

SCAPINO. What's ten years up the river when you're
with a friend?

SYLVESTRO. I can't swim.

(SYLVESTRO and SCAPINO begin to exit, going over
the bridge and across the upstage area toward the
cafe, as the HEADWAITER enters, goes down the
stairs L and up the stairs to the forestage table.)

SCAPINO. Let's have a word with Godfather. (They
exit upstage, beyond the cafe.)

The whole cast (offstage) sings as action continues.

POLLO ALL AMERICANA

Pollo All Americana,
Scampi Fritti in Brodo

Pasta Bolognese,
Pate Mayonnaise,
Capuchino Espresso

Minestrone Macaroni,
Ravioli Aux Crevette,
Caramella In Padella,
Avocado Vinaigrette.

Scallopina Valdostana
Bistecca Con Rissoto,
Pasta Bolognese
Pate Mayonnaise
Da Un Buon Appetito.

Minestrone Macaroni,
Ravioli Aux Crevette,
Caramella In Padella,
Avocado Vinaigrette.

(HEADWAITER takes spoon and fork off spaghetti
plate and rolls them in a napkin he has brought
on with him. WAITER 2 enters from cafe
yawning and stretching. He crosses to R and
takes a position on the bridge. HEADWAITER
takes fork and spoon in napkin and puts it in
breadbasket. CARLO enters from cafe and
leans against balcony post. HEADWAITER
throws basket to WAITER 2 who throws it to a
surprised CARLO who throws it through cafe
doors where it is caught by WAITER 1. They
then throw the three rolls and the wine carafe.
HEADWAITER takes wine glasses, puts them on
chair, and with great flair pulls tablecloth out
from under spaghetti plate. He throws tablecloth
to WAITER 2, who puts it over his arm.
HEADWAITER then picks up spaghetti plate, holds

it to audience as the singing in cafe stops. He
makes three turns to audience with plate high in
the air and then throws it to WAITER. He then
sits on stage steps and toasts himself with wine
glass. WAITER 2 throws plate to CARLO who
barely catches it and then throws it into cafe
where we hear it crash. After crash, singing
begins again. WAITERS and CARLO exit
quickly into cafe. Singing stops after they exit.
Enter GERONTE and ARGANTE from R.
ARGANTE crosses to stage L. GERONTE
sits on bench.)

ARGANTE. Who ever heard of such a thing. What a
thing to do. I wonder what they have to say to
me? . . . etc. . . . etc.

GERONTE (hitting umbrella on floor). What you have
just told me about your son's scandalous behavior
ruins the preparations we have made together.

ARGANTE (crossing to bench and sitting). Now don't
you worry yourself about that. I'll be responsible
for the removal of that obstacle, and I'm going
to see about it this very minute.

GERONTE. Well, my goodness gracious me, Signor
Argante, I really must say the education of
children is a matter which demands a great deal
of conscientious application.

ARGANTE. Yes, that's very true. But why bring
that up now?

GERONTE. It has just occurred to me that the bad
behavior of young people usually springs from the
bad education their fathers give them.

ARGANTE. Yes, I suppose so. . . . What exactly do
you mean by that?

GERONTE. What exactly do I mean by that?

ARGANTE. Yes.

GERONTE. That if like a responsible father you had

brought up your son properly he would not have
played this trick on you.

ARGANTE.   Charming! And we can take it that you
have brought up your son without a flaw.

GERONTE.   Without a floor? Oh, without a flaw! No
question of it.   And I should be very put out if my
son had done anything even approaching your son's
behavior.

ARGANTE.   And, oh, what if this son of yours, brought
up so properly by his responsible father, had got
into a worse mess than mine? Eh?

GERONTE.   Worse mess than . . . what do you mean?

ARGANTE.   What do I mean?

GERONTE.   What are you getting at?

ARGANTE.   What I'm getting at, Signor Geronte, is
that we shouldn't be so quick to criticize other
people's behavior. People who throw stones
should make sure the windows are boarded up
at home.

GERONTE.   I'm not very good at riddles.

ARGANTE (standing and crossing L). Well, get
someone to explain it to you then.

GERONTE (stopping ARGANTE with umbrella). You
wouldn't by any chance have heard a little something about my son?

ARGANTE.   It's quite possible.

GERONTE (standing). Well, spit it out then.

ARGANTE.   Your fellow Scapino gave me the outline.
In my own fury I missed the details, but I'm quite
sure most of Naples can fill in those for you.
(GERONTE sits.) Well, I am off to consult a
lawyer, to find out what's best to do next.
Arrivederci. (Exits L.)

GERONTE.   Arrivederci. (Stands.) What can it be?
A worse mess than his? I can't think of anything
he could do worse.

(LEANDRO starts down house left aisle.)

GERONTE. Marrying without a father's consent is
    the worst thing I can think of.
LEANDRO (entering forestage, turning to look back).
    Ciao! (Throws a kiss.) Carissima. (He runs
    UR, then sees his father and stops.)
GERONTE and LEANDRO (simultaneously). Ah-ha,
    there you are. (LEANDRO runs to embrace his
    father at C.)
LEANDRO. Father, what a delight to see you back in
    Naples.
GERONTE (refusing to embrace him, holding him off
    with umbrella). Take it easy. I've a little
    something to discuss with you first.
LEANDRO. But, Father, surely you'll let me embrace
    you.
GERONTE (holding him off with umbrella as it opens).
    Keep off, I tell you.
LEANDRO. But, surely, you'll let me show my
    happiness by my welcome.
GERONTE. Certainly, but first we have a little
    something to sort out together.
LEANDRO (crossing to left of GERONTE). Oh,
    and what may that be ?
GERONTE. Hold still and let me look you straight
    in the eye.
LEANDRO (stopping and turning). But, Father . . .
GERONTE. Look me straight in the eye.
LEANDRO (taking sunglasses off and putting in pocket).
    Very well. (Stepping face-to-face with GERONTE.)
GERONTE. What has been going on here ?
LEANDRO. Going on ?
GERONTE. Yes. What have you been doing while I've
    been away ?
LEANDRO. What would you have liked me to have

done, Father?

GERONTE.   It's not a matter of what I might have
    liked you to have done, I'm asking you what it
    is you have done. (Hits LEANDRO on arm.)

LEANDRO (as both turn front).   I don't think I've
    done anything that would give you cause for
    concern.

GERONTE.   Nothing at all?

LEANDRO.   Nothing.

GERONTE.   You're very certain.

LEANDRO.   That's because I know I've done nothing
    wrong.

GERONTE.   Scapino seems to think otherwise.

LEANDRO.   Scapino?

GERONTE.   Ha, ha, ha.   That makes you blush.

LEANDRO.   Did he tell you something about me?

GERONTE.   Did he tell me . . . this place is not
    very suitable to settle this business with all
    these people watching. We'll settle this at
    home. Go there immediately. (Hits LEANDRO's
    arm.) Don't talk to anyone on the way. (Hits
    LEANDRO's arm.) I'll be back myself in a
    moment. (Tries to hit LEANDRO again and
    misses. LEANDRO, moving away, almost falls
    into sea. GERONTE crosses down to front stage
    left.) You're a disgrace. If you've brought
    dishonor on the good name of Geronte, I'll throw
    you out and you'll never darken my door again.
    My door's quite dark enough as it is . . . (Exits
    down steps and up aisle.)

LEANDRO (now at forestage).   How could Scapino
    betray me like this? A weasel who for a hundred
    reasons ought to be the first to keep to himself
    my secrets is the first to give me away to my
    father. I could tear him into a thousand pieces
    and feed him to the fishes.

(Enter OTTAVIO and SCAPINO from cafe, the latter
     eating a mock sausage. They cross to stage R.)

OTTAVIO. Dear Scapino, I don't know how to thank
     you. Heaven smiled on me when it sent you to
     my help.
LEANDRO (running up to SCAPINO). Ah-ha, there you
     are. What ecstasy to see you again, Master
     Trickster.
SCAPINO (bowing). Oh, your servant, sir. Your
     servant. You flatter me.
LEANDRO (grabbing sausage). Don't make cruel
     jokes with me.
SCAPINO. Sir!
LEANDRO. I'll teach you a lesson. (Tries to hit
     SCAPINO with sausage. SCAPINO ducks and he
     hits OTTAVIO. SCAPINO flees L, LEANDRO in
     pursuit. OTTAVIO runs after them.)
OTTAVIO (trying to stop LEANDRO). Leandro!
LEANDRO. No, Ottavio, don't try to stop me,
     please.
SCAPINO. But, sir . . .
OTTAVIO. Calm yourself.
LEANDRO (trying to hit SCAPINO). Just let me pay
     him back.
OTTAVIO. Leandro, don't be so violent.
SCAPINO. What have I done, sir?
LEANDRO. What have you done? Traitor. (Kicking
     SCAPINO, who jumps into boat.)
OTTAVIO. Take it easy.
LEANDRO (going down steps to boat). No, Ottavio,
     I mean to make him confess here and now the
     dirty trick he's played. (Hits SCAPINO.) You
     scum, I know the game you've been up to. You
     didn't expect the story would come back to me so
     quickly. Come on, out with it, confess it was

your doing. (SCAPINO climbs out of boat and
runs R, followed by OTTAVIO.) Out with it, or
you'll never blab another secret again. (Chases
OTTAVIO and SCAPINO to stage R.)

SCAPINO. Sir, you wouldn't mutilate me with a thing
like that, would you?

LEANDRO. I would.

SCAPINO. You wouldn't.

LEANDRO. I'm waiting.

SCAPINO (putting OTTAVIO between him and
LEANDRO). Yes, sir, but, I mean, what have
I done?

LEANDRO. You know. Your conscience tells you
very well.

SCAPINO. Honestly, sir, I swear I don't know.
(LEANDRO goes for SCAPINO. OTTAVIO falls
to floor. LEANDRO cartwheels over him.)

LEANDRO. You know very well.

(First chase. SCAPINO runs down to lower
corner of forestage, then turns sharply toward
table. LEANDRO chases him all the way, while
OTTAVIO tries to intervene.)

OTTAVIO. Leandro!

SCAPINO (leaping onto chair). All right, all right.
I confess it was me who drank that small barrel
of wine someone gave you as a present a few days
ago. I entertained a few guests. It was me who
made a hole in the barrel and poured water all
over the floor to make you think the wine had run
out.

LEANDRO. So it was you who drank the wine and let
me scream at the servant girl thinking she was
to blame.

SCAPINO. Yes, sir. Yes, sir. I do hope that you
will forgive me.

LEANDRO. I'm very glad to know about that, Scapino, but it doesn't happen to be what I'm after at the moment. (Swings at SCAPINO, who runs. LEANDRO misses him and, on backswing, hits OTTAVIO.)

(Second chase begins, this time through the water. The dialogue continues during the chase. SCAPINO runs upstage across the bridge, then across the center of the stage, past the cafe, and down the steps to the water, closely pursued by LEANDRO and OTTAVIO. When SCAPINO steps into the sea, OTTAVIO and LEANDRO stop in place and say "Ech!" then they follow suit. As they go through the sea, all hold their pants legs up and lift their knees high. SCAPINO races past the boat and climbs onto the forestage from its upstage side. He skirts the table on its downstage side and runs L, finally leaping off the stage by the barrels at L and running down the aisle into the audience. OTTAVIO and LEANDRO have followed but instead of going stage L, they run to the forestage steps.)

SCAPINO. That's not it?
LEANDRO. No. It's something more serious, and I'm determined to have it.
SCAPINO. But I can't think of anything more serious, sir.
LEANDRO (going to hit him). You won't say?
SCAPINO. Oh . . .
OTTAVIO. Gently there.
SCAPINO (in audience). Look, I'm very sorry about this. All right, sir. I confess. Do you remember that little gold watch you gave to me to give to the gypsy girl you're in love with and I came back with my clothes torn to pieces and my face covered

in blood and I told you some thugs had beaten me
up and robbed me of that gold watch. (LEANDRO:
"Well?") Well, it was me, sir. I wanted the
gold watch myself.

LEANDRO. But what could you possibly want my
watch for?

SCAPINO. To see what time it was.

LEANDRO. I'm afraid you've not hit it yet.

SCAPINO. That's still not it?

LEANDRO. No, criminal. It's something more
serious still.

SCAPINO. Damnation!

(Third chase begins. SCAPINO runs out stage L
into backstage area. OTTAVIO and LEANDRO
run down the steps and follow. Then LEANDRO
runs on stage from L, looking for SCAPINO.
SCAPINO comes backing out of the cafe.
LEANDRO, seeing him, runs after him.
OTTAVIO comes out of cafe as SCAPINO leaps
back in, and LEANDRO hits him by mistake.)

OTTAVIO. Don't be so violent.

(They lock hands, spin three times in a circle;
OTTAVIO falls into sea at stage C. SCAPINO runs
around behind set to stage R. OTTAVIO clambers
up on the forestage from the rear and spits water
on himself. SCAPINO climbs ladder at stage R
and enters balcony. OTTAVIO walks up to the
laughing LEANDRO, who is still by the bench,
and spits water in his face. LEANDRO runs
after a laughing SCAPINO and climbs up to
balcony. LEANDRO chases SCAPINO off
balcony where SCAPINO hangs on rope.)

SCAPINO. All right, sir, I confess it. Do you

remember that ghost you met on the stairs a few
weeks ago and nearly broke your neck falling
backwards into the cellar running away?

LEANDRO. Well? (With SCAPINO.) You were
the ghost.

SCAPINO. I was the ghost, sir . . . Just to frighten
you a little bit to stop you from staying up all
night keeping us running around as you used to
do. (LEANDRO hits SCAPINO with sausage.
SCAPINO falls off rope.)

LEANDRO. I'll remember all this at a proper time
and place, Scapino, but in the meantime come
to the point and confess exactly what you told my
father.

SCAPINO. Told your father?

LEANDRO. Yes, my father.

SCAPINO. I haven't so much as seen him since his
return.

LEANDRO. You've not?

SCAPINO. No, sir.

LEANDRO. Really?

SCAPINO. They'll tell you the same thing -- I
haven't seen him.

LEANDRO. I have it from his own lips that . . .

SCAPINO. Well, excuse the expression, but his lips
are not telling the truth. (Sound of telephone
bell ringing.)

(CARLO enters from cafe with old-fashioned, cordless
telephone and crosses R.)

CARLO. Pronto, pronto. (LEANDRO comes down
from balcony. SCAPINO goes and sits by the
water, while OTTAVIO comes down to CARLO.)
Signore, signore, terrible news. They're carrying
her off.

LEANDRO (at bottom of ladder). Who? (Runs to CARLO.)

CARLO (listening on telephone). The gypsies are on
     the point of running away with Zerbinetta.
     (LEANDRO and OTTAVIO,on the sides of CARLO,
     take three steps forward.) She's crying.
     (LEANDRO grabs receiver. OTTAVIO holds
     base of telephone.)
LEANDRO. She never cries. (CARLO gets choked
     on wire between base and receiver.)
CARLO (grabbing telephone back). She's crying now.
     (Listens.) She says that if you don't get them
     the money the gypsies have demanded for her
     within two hours, she will be gone from you
     forever. (Hangs up telephone.)
LEANDRO. In two hours?
CARLO (listening again). In two hours? ("Si.")
     Si, two hours. (Hangs up telephone. LEANDRO
     takes telephone and gives sausage to CARLO.
     CARLO gives sausage to OTTAVIO, takes
     telephone and goes back to cafe. OTTAVIO
     gives sausage to LEANDRO, who at first thinks
     it's the telephone and then throws it, hitting
     CARLO. A squeak as it hits.)
LEANDRO (moving toward SCAPINO). Pronto, pronto,
     pronto, pronto . . . Dearest Scapino, give me
     your help. (SCAPINO escapes toward balcony.
     He fakes crying.)
SCAPINO. "Dearest Scapino"! I'm dearest Scapino
     now that you need me.
LEANDRO (moving L, then returning to bench). I'll
     forgive you anything you've told me and anything
     worse you've done.
SCAPINO. No, no, don't forgive me anything. Strangle
     me, stick a knife in me, beat me to death with a
     club. I'll enjoy every minute while you're killing
     me. (Kneels.)
LEANDRO. No, I beg you to save my life in saving
     my love. (Kneels.)

SCAPINO. Just finish me off quickly, that's all I
     ask. (On hands and knees.)
LEANDRO. You're too deaf to me. I need your
     genius. (On hands and knees.)
SCAPINO. Kill me. (Lies down.)
LEANDRO. No. (Lies down.)
SCAPINO. Just kill me. (Pushes up on hands and
     feet.)
LEANDRO. No. (Pushes up on hands and feet.)
SCAPINO. Just get it over with. (Flips onto back.)
LEANDRO. No. (Flips onto back.)
OTTAVIO (lying on his back next to SCAPINO).
     Scapino, you must do something to help.
SCAPINO (raising his head, then standing). What?
     After the way he insulted me?
LEANDRO (kneeling). Forget all that, I beg you,
     and give me your help.
OTTAVIO (kneeling). I join my petition to his.
SCAPINO (crossing downstage). I can still feel that
     insult deep down in here.
OTTAVIO. Put your pride on one side. (SCAPINO
     puts his pride on one side.)
LEANDRO (standing and crossing to SCAPINO, who
     moves away). Scapino, are you going to
     abandon me? In this cruel extremity? I was
     wrong. I admit that.
SCAPINO (crossing into forestage, approaching table).
     To treat me like a rogue, a villain, a scoundrel.
LEANDRO. I am more sorry than I can say . . .
SCAPINO (leaning on table). Yes, but . . . to hit me
     over the head . . . in public . . . with a . . .
     sausage.
LEANDRO. I beg your pardon with all my heart.
     And if that's not enough, I'll get down on my
     knees -- (Kneeling.) -- there, Scapino, and beg
     you once again to help me.
OTTAVIO (kneeling next to LEANDRO). You can't

leave him now, Scapino. (They cry and beg
SCAPINO, who milks it and makes them fall.)
SCAPINO. Well, yes. You get up. But next time
don't be so quick with your accusations.
LEANDRO (he and OTTAVIO still kneeling). Will
you get us out of this mess?
SCAPINO. I'll think about it.
LEANDRO. Well, you know time is pressing.
SCAPINO. Well, how much do you need?
LEANDRO. Five hundred thousand lire.
SCAPINO. And you?
OTTAVIO. Two hundred thousand.
SCAPINO (going upstage). Good, I shall get these
out of your dads. (LEANDRO and OTTAVIO
stand. To OTTAVIO.) As to yours, the plan's
already made. (To LEANDRO.) And as for
yours, first-class miser though he is, there'll
be even less trouble. He's not exactly an
Einstein. He's the sort of fella you can con
into almost anything.
LEANDRO. How dare you!
SCAPINO. Now don't get upset. You know there's
not the slightest resemblance between you and
him.   And you know perfectly well that every-
body knows he's only your father because he
happened to be married to your mother at the
time.
LEANDRO. Scapino!
ARGANTE (offstage L). Of all the ridiculous behavior.
LEANDRO. Shush, Scapino!
SCAPINO. But here comes your father, Ottavio.
We'll start the deal with him since he's here
first. You get along and tell Sylvestro to come
at a trot ready to play his part. (Exit OTTAVIO
and LEANDRO into cafe. They peek out until
ARGANTE passes, then duck out of sight.)

(ARGANTE enters L and makes a long cross to R.)

ARGANTE (to himself, crossing to stage R). No good
    sense . . . no consideration. To jump headlong
    into marriage like this. Oh, the follies of youth.
SCAPINO (under stage R balcony). Your servant,
    signor.
ARGANTE. How do, Scapino.
SCAPINO. You're having a little think about your
    son's situation, are you?
ARGANTE (crossing downstage). I must admit it's
    put me in a state of fury.
SCAPINO (following him). Life, sir, is full of
    disappointments. It's best to be prepared for
    them.
ARGANTE (at forestage L). That's all very well,
    but this foolish marriage has spoiled all our
    plans, and I'm not going to stand for it. And
    I've already been to see about getting it
    dissolved. (Goes down the stairs.)
SCAPINO (at center of forestage). No, sir, if you'll
    only listen to me, you'll find another way of
    settling this. You know what going to law means
    in this country? You'll find yourself stuck into
    so many complications and costs . . . (ARGANTE
    comes up onto forestage again.)
ARGANTE. Costs! That's true. That's very true.
    But what other way is there?
SCAPINO (offering ARGANTE a seat, which he takes).
    I think I've one. I've just been chatting to the
    brother of the girl Ottavio's married. He's one
    of these roughnecks, one of these toughs who stand
    around the street corners poking people on the
    nose, beating them with chains, talking about
    nothing but punching and slashing and shooting,
    standing there with cut-throat razors waiting for
    streakers, and thinks no more of killing a bloke

than drinking a glass of wine. I got him round
to talking about the marriage. I dropped a hint
to him how easy it would be to dissolve it on
account of the gun at the ceremony, and how
your influence in the city, your bank balance and
your powerful friends would help you along in
court. Anyway, I got him to listen to a little
proposal I made for settling the whole thing for
a small consideration, and he agrees that the
marriage should be dissolved providing he gets
the money. (Goes back up to bridge.)

ARGANTE (standing). And how much did he ask?

SCAPINO. Ooh, at first, a fantastic sum.

ARGANTE. Well, tell me.

SCAPINO. Oh, you wouldn't believe it.

ARGANTE (going to foot of bridge). But tell me what.

SCAPINO. He said . . . he said . . . he wouldn't
settle for less than five or six hundred thousand
lire.

ARGANTE. Five or six hundred . . . (On bridge,
beside SCAPINO.) The devil seize him. Does
he think I'm an idiot?

SCAPINO (imitating ARGANTE behind his back).
That's just what I said to him. I said to him,
"Do you think that man is an idiot?" I said
you weren't as much an idiot as you looked and
after a lot more arguing he agrees to settle for
. . . enough to pay off his landlady so he can
collect his luggage — a mere two hundred thousand
lire.

ARGANTE. Two hundred thousand lire?

SCAPINO. Yes.

ARGANTE (walking about forestage in a rage).
Come on, we'll go to court. (He goes down
forestage steps and up the steps L toward cafe.)

SCAPINO. Oh, oh, think, sir.

ARGANTE (going up stairs by the boat). I'll go to

Part I   Scapino!   Page 47

court. (SCAPINO approaches ARGANTE by crossing bridge and going L.)

SCAPINO. Now don't go jumping head-first into . . .

ARGANTE (continuing off L). I'll go to court.

SCAPINO. You know that going to court will cost you money.

(ARGANTE runs back on stage.)

ARGANTE. Money? (He stops by the steps of the boat landing.)

SCAPINO (taking ARGANTE by the shoulder and running him back on forestage). Not to mention the little bits here and there for greasing of palms. Give the man the money and you've settled the whole thing.

ARGANTE. But two hundred thousand lire.

SCAPINO. Yes, and you'll make a profit.

ARGANTE (turning to SCAPINO). Profit! (SCAPINO offers ARGANTE a chair again, which he takes. SCAPINO sits opposite him.)

SCAPINO. Yes, a profit. I've just been doing a quick calculation in my head of all the legal costs and I've worked out that in giving your man two hundred thousand lire you'll save at least a hundred and fifty thousand over and above that without reckoning all the worries and anxieties, time wasting and vexation you'll cause yourself. Even if it saved you all the cheeky things the lawyers will write about you that could well appear in the *Women's Wear Daily* , it could be worth three hundred thousand not to go to law.

ARGANTE. I don't care a damn, I defy any lawyer to make an idiot of me.

SCAPINO (standing). . . . Then do what you will, sir. (Walks away.)

(SCAPINO whistles for SYLVESTRO, who enters cafe
    balcony L in leathers with a bicycle chain.)

SCAPINO.   . . . but if I were you I'd avoid the law.
ARGANTE.   I'm not giving away two hundred thousand
    lire.
SCAPINO.   Ah! (Getting ARGANTE to look at cafe
    balcony.)
SYLVESTRO (on balcony). Hey, hey, Scapino, come
    and show me where this rat Argante, Ottavio's
    father, is. (Exits balcony.)
SCAPINO (returning to table). Why, old chap . . .
    Sir, do you know who that is? That's the brother
    of the girl Ottavio married; who stands on street
    corners going . . .

(Enter SYLVESTRO from cafe, imitating a bouncing
    thug.)

SYLVESTRO (crossing to C). You deaf or something?
    Come and show me where that rat Argante,
    Ottavio's father, is.
SCAPINO (as he and ARGANTE stand). Why, old chap?
SYLVESTRO. I've just heard he's gonna take me to
    court, and dissolve by law the marriage of my
    sister.
SCAPINO. I don't know whether he intends to do that,
    but I do know he won't pay you two hundred
    thousand lire. He says it's far too much.
    (SYLVESTRO moves in and back again, swinging
    his fists and chain. ARGANTE tries to run off L.
    SCAPINO stops him.)
SYLVESTRO (continuing to pace and swing chain).
    I'll kill him . . . Off with his head . . . Off
    with his appendages. If I find him, I'll make
    mincemeat of him, even if I get the chair for
    it. (Banging into R chair.)

SCAPINO. But, sir, Ottavio's father has guts and
    maybe he won't be frightened of you.

SYLVESTRO (coming to lower end of bridge). Him?
    Him? Blood and giblets. If he was standing
    there now, I'd wrap my chain 'round his chops
    in no time at all. (Sees ARGANTE.) Who's that
    man there?

SCAPINO (pushing ARGANTE forward toward
    SYLVESTRO). Oh, this man, that's not him;
    that's not him.

SYLVESTRO. Are you sure it isn't a friend of
    Argante?

SCAPINO. A friend? No, no. This man is his
    deadliest enemy.

SYLVESTRO. His deadliest enemy? (As ARGANTE
    makes like a deadly enemy, clawing.)

SCAPINO. Yes.

SYLVESTRO. Well, you old sonofabitch, glad to'meet
    you. So you're a deadly enemy of that fellow
    Argante, eh?

SCAPINO (going to table and leaning on it). Yes,
    I'll answer for him.

SYLVESTRO. Shake, buster, shake. (ARGANTE
    shakes all over.) I give you my word, I'll swear
    on my honor, by the chain I carry, by the razor
    in my pocket, by all the saints -- (Spitting in his
    own hand, and crossing to ARGANTE.) -- that
    before this day's finished I'll rid you of that
    sniveling scoundrel, that stool pigeon Argante.
    You can depend on me. (They shake hands.
    Both react and wipe off spit.)

SCAPINO. But, sir, violence is against the law in
    this country.

SYLVESTRO. What do I care? What have I got to
    lose?

SCAPINO. But he has friends and relatives who'll
    protect him against you.

SYLVESTRO. That's just what I want. Gaawd.
(Moving back upstage. He swings chain and does
a mock attack as though there are lots of people
around him.) Off with his head; right across the
belly. If only he was here right now with all his
friends and relations! Just let him get near with
thirty policemen! Let 'em all come, truncheons,
pistols, and all! (He stands on his guard.) Okay,
you guys, fight to the finish. Come on, rats, fight
to kill. No prisoners. Slash! (Leaps toward
table, miming fight.) Bang! Strangle! Worms!
Chickens! If that's what you want, I'll give you
your bellyful. One down, pow, pow, pop, two
down, pow, pow. (Threatens ARGANTE and
SCAPINO.) Frightened, eh? (Hitting chain on
table.)

SCAPINO. Sir, we're on your side, sir.

SYLVESTRO (moving back upstage). Well, that just
shows you what happens to anybody who gets on
the wrong side of me. (Bangs into bench, puts
his hands up.) I beg your pardon. (Turns, sees
it's the bench, hits it with chain, exits cafe.)

SCAPINO (moving R). That just shows you how many
men can be killed for a mere two hundred
thousand lire. Oi vey, I'm off! (Exits stage R
stairs.)

ARGANTE (crossing to bridge, trembling).
Sca . . . Sca . . . Sca . . . Sca . . . Sca . . .
Sca . . . Sca . . . Scapino!

(SCAPINO re-enters, up stairs.)

SCAPINO (moving to ARGANTE). Pino . . .
pino . . . pino, sir . . . pino.

ARGANTE. I've changed my mind. I think I'll give
him the money.

SCAPINO. Sir, I'm delighted, for your sake.

ARGANTE (taking out wallet). Let's go and find him;
  I've got the money with me.
SCAPINO. No, sir, all you have to do is give the
  money to me. It's not possible for you to meet
  him, not after pretending to be somebody else;
  and I'm afraid knowing you've tricked him, he
  might decide to ask for more.
ARGANTE. True, true, but I'd feel a lot happier to
  see what happened to my money.
SCAPINO. Don't you trust me, sir?
ARGANTE. Oh, no, no, it's not that, but . . .
SCAPINO (returning to stairs). Now, sir, either I'm
  a rogue or I'm an honest man; one or the other.
  Why should I want to trick you? It's only to help
  you and my master that I'm risking all this.
  (ARGANTE moves down to him.) If you don't
  trust me, then I'll wash my hands of the whole
  thing and you'd better find someone else to do
  your dirty work for you.
ARGANTE (trying to give him the money). No, you
  take the money.
SCAPINO (refusing it). No, sir, I'll be very happy
  if you give it to someone else.
ARGANTE. Take it! I beg you.
SCAPINO. No. How do you know I won't trick you
  out of your money?
ARGANTE. For God's sake, take it. Don't make me
  argue any more . . . I'll go and wait for you at
  home. (Hands money to SCAPINO, goes upstage
  and across toward cafe.)
SCAPINO. I'll be there shortly. (ARGANTE exits upstage.)

(SYLVESTRO enters cafe balcony.)

SYLVESTRO. Ciao!
SCAPINO. Ciao! (Repeat Ciao!) One down, one to
  go. (Sits at table counting money.)

SYLVESTRO. Hey, here he comes now.

(SYLVESTRO exits into cafe as GERONTE approaches
     from stage R aisle.)

SCAPINO (jumping up, putting money away). Oh,
     God, heaven's got them queueing up today.
     (Running about, pretending he hasn't seen
     GERONTE.) Poor old fellow! Poor old Geronte.
     Poor old chap. What'll he do?
GERONTE (onto forestage via steps). What's he saying
     about me? With a face like a lemon.
SCAPINO (running upstage and to bench). Can anyone
     tell me where to find poor, poor Signor Geronte?
GERONTE (going upstage as SCAPINO runs down).
     What's the matter, Scapino? (They have passed
     each other, SCAPINO now being at lower edge of
     forestage.)
SCAPINO (running L). If only I could find him to tell
     him about this terrible disaster.
GERONTE. What on earth is it?
SCAPINO. I've searched everywhere for him, but all
     in vain.
GERONTE (down to bridge). I'm here! . . . It's me.
SCAPINO (running to upstage edge of forestage and
     peering over). Maybe he is hiding under the quay
     and nobody can find him.
GERONTE (coming up behind him and poking him with
     umbrella). Hey, are you deaf?
SCAPINO. Sir! It's impossible to find you anywhere,
     sir.
GERONTE. I've been standing right behind you for
     the past hour. What on earth is it, whatever it is?
SCAPINO. Sir.
GERONTE. What?
SCAPINO. Sir, your son . . .
GERONTE. Go on. My son . . .

SCAPINO. Your son has got himself mixed up in the
    most extraordinary business in the whole world.
GERONTE. Whatever's that?
SCAPINO (joining GERONTE on bridge). Well, I saw
    him a short while ago looking upset, very un-
    happy, at something you must have said to him,
    in which for no good reason you managed to get
    me involved; and seeking to take his mind off
    his troubles, I took him for a walk along the
    quayside. (He walks GERONTE upstage.) There
    we were, admiring the boats, one of them in
    particular, a beautiful motor-yacht, when up
    came a young fellow, Turkish he was, what a
    delight, shook us by the hand and invited us on
    board. (They sit on bench.) So on we went.
    We ate the most beautiful food, and drank wine
    such as you've never tasted.
GERONTE. Well, how did this make you feel so bad?
SCAPINO. Just a minute, just a minute, sir! While
    we were eating and drinking, he ordered the
    boat to put to sea and when we were a good way
    from the harbor he threw me overboard into the
    skiff -- (Jumps into boat.) -- and sent me to
    tell you that if you don't send him by return by
    me five hundred thousand lire he'll kidnap your
    son and sail him off to Algiers.
GERONTE (jumping up). What the devil . . . five
    hundred thousand lire!
SCAPINO. Yes, sir, and not only that, he's given
    me only two hours to get it. No, I'm a liar, one
    hour and fifty minutes.
GERONTE. Oh, that terror of a Turk, he'll be the
    death of me.
SCAPINO (climbing out of boat). You must tell me,
    sir, how to rescue your son who you love so
    tenderly from a fate worse than death.
GERONTE (stamping foot). What the devil was he

doing on board that board?

SCAPINO. Well, he didn't realize this was going to
   happen, did he, sir?

GERONTE. Off with you, Scapino, off with you, and
   tell that Turk I'll send the police after him.

SCAPINO (running off, then stopping on the bridge).
   The police, sir, what a good idea. . . . The
   police? In the middle of the ocean? Look, you
   must be having a joke with me.

GERONTE (stamping foot). What the devil was he
   doing on board that boat?

SCAPINO. Well . . . ah . . . some people have bad
   luck, sir.

GERONTE. Scapino, the time has come when you
   must play the part of a faithful servant.

SCAPINO (returning to GERONTE). Yes, sir.

GERONTE. Go along, and ask this Turk to send me
   back my son, and tell him I've sent you to take
   my son's place until I've got enough cash together.

SCAPINO (running off again and then again stopping
   on bridge). What an idea . . . what an idea,
   sir! . . . Do you really know what you're talking
   about?

GERONTE. No . . .

SCAPINO. Do you expect that Turk to have so little
   savvy as to swap your son for a wretch like me?

GERONTE (stamping foot). What the devil was he
   doing on board that boat?

SCAPINO (imitating GERONTE). Well, he didn't
   know it was going to happen, did he? Just think,
   sir, he only gave me an hour and a half.

GERONTE. You say he asks . . .

SCAPINO (crossing to GERONTE with hand out for
   money). Five hundred thousand lire.

GERONTE. Five hundred thousand lire.

SCAPINO. Yes.

GERONTE. Has he no conscience?

SCAPINO. Certainly. The conscience of a Turk.
    (Both laugh, then to audience:)
SCAPINO and GERONTE. That's not funny!
GERONTE. Does he think that money like that is
    just picked up in the gutter?
SCAPINO. Some people have no business sense.
GERONTE. But what the devil was he doing on board
    that boat?
SCAPINO (moving downstage). Yes . . . Yes . . .
    Quite right. But one doesn't read fortunes, does
    one, sir? Look . . . Come on, let's get it over
    with.
GERONTE (taking key out of pocket and going to
    SCAPINO). All right. Here's the key of my
    closet.
SCAPINO (meeting GERONTE). Good. (Takes the
    key.)
GERONTE. Open it.
SCAPINO. What? The key?
GERONTE. The closet.
SCAPINO. Oh, very good.
GERONTE. Inside you'll find a little hook. On the
    hook you'll find a big key which unlocks the attic.
    Inside you'll find a larger key which is the key to
    my secret hidey hole. Go in there and you'll
    see a large brass bedstead. On the bed there is
    a mattress. Lift it up, roll it over, sell it and
    use the money to ransom my son.
SCAPINO. Sell it. You wouldn't get a hundred lire
    for a mattress, and please think how little time
    there is.
GERONTE. What the devil was he doing on board
    that boat?
SCAPINO. Quite right; but forget the boat. Drop the
    boat. Because by this time you've almost lost
    your son. (Gives key back to GERONTE and goes
    L. He bursts into tears.) Poor, poor, poor

fellow. I may never see you again. They're
sailing you off to Algiers to a fate we wot not of.
But heaven's my witness — (Falls on knees.) --
I've done all I could, and there's none to blame
but a hard-hearted father.

GERONTE (crossing R). Don't strain yourself,
Scapino. I'll go and get the money.

SCAPINO (now by the boat). Then hurry, sir. I
tremble lest the clock strikes.

GERONTE (stopping under the balcony and turning).
Was it four hundred thousand you said?

SCAPINO. No, no, five hundred thousand.

GERONTE. Five hundred thousand?

SCAPINO. Yes.

GERONTE. What the devil was he doing on board
that boat?

SCAPINO. Quite right, but hurry up.

GERONTE. Blast that boat.

SCAPINO (to audience). That boat's going to give
him a heart attack.

GERONTE (crossing to SCAPINO). Here, Scapino.
I've remembered someone's paid me money . . .
I never dreamed it'd be leaving me so soon.
Here, take it. Ransom my son. (Puts money on
SCAPINO's outstretched hand.)

SCAPINO. Sir.

GERONTE. But tell that Turk he's a devil. (More
money.)

SCAPINO. Yes, sir!

GERONTE. A murderer. (More money.)

SCAPINO. Certainly, sir.

GERONTE. A money-grabber. (More money.)

SCAPINO. Just you leave it to me, sir.

GERONTE (more money). And if I ever catch him
I'll have my revenge on him. (Takes all money
and goes R.)

SCAPINO (calling after him). Just a minute, sir. . . .

Where's the money?

GERONTE. I gave it to you.

SCAPINO. No, no. . . . You put it back in your wallet.

GERONTE. I put it back in my wallet?

SCAPINO. You put it back in your wallet.

GERONTE. In my wallet . . . I put it back in my wallet. . . . (Crossing to SCAPINO and giving him the money, wallet and all.) Ah, it's grief disturbs my senses.

SCAPINO. That's plain to see.

GERONTE (crossing R). What the devil was he doing on board that boat? Blast the boat. That terror of a Turk, he'll be the death of me. (Stops a moment, facing audience. SCAPINO stands on bench, encouraging audience to join in.)

SCAPINO and GERONTE. What the devil was he doing on board that boat?

GERONTE. I hate Turks. (Exits R.)

SCAPINO. I'm not through with you yet, you old miser. I'll pay you back in another form of coin for the tale you told about me to your son. (Crosses downstage to bridge.)

(Enter OTTAVIO and LEANDRO from L in bathing suits, flippers, masks, snorkels. They jump in sea and swim to SCAPINO.)

OTTAVIO (up on bridge, removing mask and flippers). Well, Scapino, any success? (LEANDRO jumps out of water farther upstage and takes off mask and flippers.)

SCAPINO (to OTTAVIO). Two hundred thousand lire.

OTTAVIO (standing and taking money). I'm wild with happiness.

LEANDRO. And have you done anything to save my love from disaster?

SCAPINO (to LEANDRO). Sir, for you, I could do
    nothing . . .

LEANDRO (running into cafe and up to balcony).
    Then I must end it all. Life means nothing to
    me without my lovely Zerbinetta. (At balcony,
    climbing over rail, threatening to jump.) What
    else can I do? I must end it all. (OTTAVIO
    and SCAPINO run to L, look up at balcony.)

SCAPINO. What's he talking about? . . . No, no.
    Wait. Take it easy. I was only joking. . . .
    Sir, stop it. Here, will this settle your
    difficulties? (Holding out money.)

LEANDRO. You've made life worth living.

SCAPINO (to OTTAVIO). Get him down. (OTTAVIO
    helps LEANDRO down. SCAPINO holds out
    money, then pulls it back.) On one condition.
    That you allow me a little revenge on your father
    for this trick he's played on me.

LEANDRO (reaching for money). Anything you like.

SCAPINO (pulling money back). You swear it, in
    front of witnii?

LEANDRO. Yes.

SCAPINO (giving LEANDRO money). Five hundred
    thousand lire. (Exits cafe.)

LEANDRO. Come on, let's go and buy the lovely
    creature that I love.

OTTAVIO. My lovely Giacinta. (Puts mask back on.)

LEANDRO. My lovely Zerbinetta. (Puts mask back
    on. They jump into sea, lie down as if in water.
    Then both stand, lift masks, and shout their own
    sound effects.)

OTTAVIO and LEANDRO. Splash! (They bow and
    swim off stage L.)

END OF PART ONE

the intermission

HEADWAITER and WAITER 1 enter from cafe, move
bench into Part Two position and cross to the table
and chairs on forestage. WAITRESS enters yawning,
puts five coins in jukebox and starts music as she
did previously. She moves chair from table L to
right of jukebox and returns to cafe. WAITERS start
the following routine: wearily they put the chairs on
top of the table and carry table, chairs and all upstage.
As they run into obstacles (steps, ramps, etc.) they
can't pass, they put table down, remove chairs, carry
table and chairs separately over obstacle, and then
put chairs back on table carrying the whole load to
the next obstacle where they repeat the process.
WAITRESS enters eating a large hero-type sandwich
and sits in chair by jukebox watching them. Moving
down the last obstacle (stage L ramp) the WAITERS,
not judging the weight of the table correctly, lose
control and crash through the cafe doors. They come
back out, put table and chairs upstage of cafe.
HEADWAITER, going back into cafe, notices
WAITRESS and "giving her a look" tells her to get
up and motions WAITER 1 to put chair with the others.
HEADWAITER exits. WAITER 1, "coming on" to
WAITRESS throughout, takes chair with one hand -
showing his strength - and puts it away. He goes back
to WAITRESS and she begins stroking and massaging
his right arm, which he raises in the air flexing its
muscle. The WAITRESS crosses by him leading him
toward cafe. He follows with arm held in flexed
position. At cafe entrance, she turns to him, nods
her head and both exit quickly into cafe.

part two

(The jukebox is still playing. Seagulls are heard.
The stage is clear. The NURSE enters the
auditorium from the front of the house with the
last of the audience, and moves down the stage
R aisle toward the stage; crosses in front of the
forestage to the stage L stairs by the boat; walks
up the stairs and looks in the garbage barrel.
HEADWAITER and WAITER 1 come into the cafe
balcony and begin playing a game, one hiding
chalk in his closed hands, the other trying to
guess which hand it's in. The NURSE tiptoes
through the sea toward the forestage. WAITERS
stop game and watch NURSE.   NURSE wipes
muck off shoes and crosses to upstage center of
forestage, where she leans over and looks into
sea, then looks behind her at audience and fixes
her dress. She then crosses to bridge.
WAITRESS enters from cafe, eating the last of
her sandwich, and leans against downstage post
of cafe balcony watching NURSE. Now upstage
of bridge, the NURSE hears a whistle. It comes
from the cafe balcony. NURSE thinks it's from
the audience; stops, turns, makes a quiet "puss"
at someone. Receives no reactions and crosses
L toward cafe. In front of cafe she sees
WAITRESS, stops, crosses herself, turns
around, crosses to bench, takes out a hanky,
cleans bench and sits. WAITERS return to
game. CARLO enters balcony, begins participating

in game. WAITER 1 sides with CARLO, loses
and smacks CARLO on the shoulder. The sound
of guitar strumming is heard as SCAPINO enters
balcony with guitar. The seagulls fade. SCAPINO
is about to start singing "O Sole Mio"; CARLO
breaks out into song first:

O SOLE MIO

O Sole Mio (CARLO sings by himself)
Chow Chow Bambino
Three Pounds Per Kilo
Serra Serra

Pastrami, Frank Dunlopillo (SCAPINO and
        WAITER 1 join CARLO)
Ajax et Brillo
An' Tony Quinn

La Dolche Vita
Sophia Ponte
Moonlight In Vermonte
Serra Serra
Chinzano et Mia Farrow
Until tomarrow
Chow Chow for Now
        Ole! (A shout)

LEANDRO and OTTAVIO enter from cafe dancing
together and drinking chianti. They stop dancing
left of bench. LEANDRO drinks. OTTAVIO
takes bottle, drinks and leads LEANDRO off R
dangling the bottle. Song ends. SCAPINO
continues strumming guitar as he and WAITERS
hum slow version of "Minestrone Macaroni."
As song ends, CARLO leaves balcony, runs down
stairs and enters from cafe, ice cream box hanging

from neck, scoop in hand. "Gelati, Gelati!"
WAITRESS enters cafe. CARLO crosses R.
"Gelati molta, molta freddo." He stops right
of NURSE. She signals for an ice cream, stands,
crosses to him. He opens ice cream box; she
points inside; he whispers in her ear. She reacts
violently, hits him on head with handbag and exits
to cafe. CARLO crosses L and down steps by
boat; "Gelati, Gelati, chocolata, vanilla, molta
flavores, cento flavores, Baskein Robins."
GIACINTA, ZERBINETTA and SYLVESTRO enter
R humming the same as men of balcony and miming
mandolin play with forefinger in front of mouth.
GIACINTA turns to cross down bridge to forestage;
SYLVESTRO to bench and sit; ZERBINETTA to
right of bench. CARLO crosses to forestage:
"Chocolata a fudge ripple"; seeing GIACINTA:
"Gelati, signorina." They cross and meet at
upstage center of forestage. CARLO opens gelati
box. GIACINTA looks in, points to a flavor, and
CARLO fixes her a cone. He starts to give it
to her, looks at her breasts, reaches into box
with scoop and puts another scoop on cone and
gives it to her. He backs away from her, she
sits up left corner of forestage and ZERBINETTA
crosses down to bridge. CARLO, moving away
from GIACINTA, takes out cone for next customer
with his right hand. As he turns, the cone is crushed
on ZERBINETTA's left breast. He takes out
another cone, saying "Hagen Daze," fixes some
ice cream on it, and gives cone to her singing
"Hagen Daze are here again" and backs upstage
still looking at ZERBINETTA who sits above
bridge. As he reaches the bench he takes out a
dixie cup and bangs it against SYLVESTRO's face.
SYLVESTRO takes the cup. CARLO puts out his
hand for money. SYLVESTRO takes lid off cup

and puts it sticky-side down on CARLO's outstretched hand. CARLO, still looking at
ZERBINETTA, puts lid in his chest pocket,
crosses L, bangs gelati box into SYLVESTRO,
and finally, still looking at ZERBINETTA,
walks *[gelati box first]* into cafe wall, gelati
box hitting him in groin. He doubles over and
exits into cafe. SCAPINO and WAITERS stop
humming and exit balcony. *[Following scene
should have a quiet romantic atmosphere.]*)

SYLVESTRO. Yes, and your two young men have
  agreed that you should stay together, and I am
  carrying out the order they have given me.
GIACINTA (eating ice cream; to ZERBINETTA). Such
  an order does nothing but please me. I am happy
  to have you as my companion, and it shall not be
  my fault if the friendship between those we love
  is not echoed between us two.

(SCAPINO enters from cafe, takes ice cream from
  SYLVESTRO, crosses R and sits in chair at
  table R.)

ZERBINETTA (eating ice cream). I agree, and I am
  not someone to refuse an offer of friendship.
SCAPINO. And when that offer is love?
ZERBINETTA. Love is another matter. There is
  a little more risk and I'm not so brave.
SCAPINO. Yes, well, I wish you'd take that risk for
  my master now. What he has just done for you
  should make you brave enough.
ZERBINETTA. What he has just done is not quite
  enough to convince me. We're just good friends.
  (Laughs.) I may be always smiling and full of
  laughter, but for all my laughing, I am serious
  on certain matters and your master mistakes

himself if he thinks his having bought me means
he owns me. He will have to fortify his love with
certain ceremonies thought necessary on these
occasions. (GIACINTA crosses and sits in prow
of boat.)

SCAPINO. That's just what he intends to do. His
intentions are strictly honorable. If a sinful
thought had entered his head, do you think I
would be mixed up in the business?

ZERBINETTA. I long to believe you, but I can see
certain objections coming from his father.

SCAPINO. Well, we'll soon sort those out.

GIACINTA (to ZERBINETTA). The similarity of our
adventures should make us still more friends;
we both suffer the same apprehensions, and are
exposed to the same misfortunes. Well, cheer
up, we're both in the same boat.

ZERBINETTA. But at least you have the advantage
of knowing who were your parents, and that one
day you can find them again; they can consent to
your marriage and set everything to rights. But
what I am makes it impossible for me to gain
the favor of his father, who respects only money.

GIACINTA. But at least you have the advantage that
your lover is not tempted to make another
marriage.

ZERBINETTA. A change of mind is the least to fear
in a lover. It's natural to believe one's attractions
will keep their interest. The real enemy is an
interfering father, for whom one's attractions
have no interest at all. Heigho.

GIACINTA. Heigh . . . ho!

SYLVESTRO. Heigh . . . ho!

GIACINTA. What crosses we true lovers must bear.
(GIACINTA, ZERBINETTA and SYLVESTRO sigh
with mouths open.) How delicious to be in love
-- (Sighs.) -- with nothing to disturb the beating

of two hearts together. (Sighs. SCAPINO laughs
crudely and stands.)

SCAPINO (crossing downstage to center of forestage).
Don't delude yourself. A peaceful love affair is
a boring one. You need your ups and downs.
Troubles in love make us appreciate the pleasures
and make us love even more. (GIACINTA and
ZERBINETTA sigh.)

ZERBINETTA (crossing down to SCAPINO). Enough,
Scapino; help us forget our troubles by making
us laugh.

GIACINTA. Mmm. (She also comes to forestage.)

SYLVESTRO. Yes.

SCAPINO. No, no, no.

ZERBINETTA. Tell us the story of how you got the
money out of the old miser.

SCAPINO. No, they heard it.

ZERBINETTA. Oh, come on. (Girls tickle his legs.)

SCAPINO. Stop it. Look, it's all right at rehearsal;
but not on the night . . . Now, I told you, didn't
I . . . Sylvestro can . . . (ZERBINETTA tickles
him again.) . . . Cut your nails . . . Look,
Sylvestro can tell you that story as well as I.
At the moment I'm trying to think up a little
revenge on old Geronte. (The girls walk up and
cross stage to area above boat.)

SYLVESTRO (moving quickly to SCAPINO). Why,
just when we're all happy, do you want to get
yourself mixed up in another load of trouble?

SCAPINO. Because it makes me happier still to risk
my chance.

SYLVESTRO. I've told you before, you'll give up that
plan if you'll take any notice of me.

SCAPINO. Who takes any notice of you?

SYLVESTRO. Now why the devil do you need to amuse
yourself in that way?

SCAPINO. And why the devil do you need to worry

about it?

SYLVESTRO. 'Cause I don't like to see you, unless it's a real case of necessity, getting yourself a good hiding.

SCAPINO. Look, it will be my good hiding, not yours.

SYLVESTRO (crossing upstage and to girls). All right, all right. Your hiding's your own affair.

SCAPINO. Look, I've never been stopped by danger. I just can't stand those boasters who are so busy working out the risks they are going to take, they don't take any.

ZERBINETTA. Hey, Scapino, we'll be needing your help.

SCAPINO. Yes, well, I'll be along in a couple of shakes of a . . .

ZERBINETTA. A what?

SCAPINO. How's your father? [An English expression meaning, "Whatever you want it to be."]

SYLVESTRO (exiting upstage with GIACINTA and ZERBINETTA). Ciao!

SCAPINO. Ciao!

OTHERS. Ciao!

SCAPINO. Ciao!

OTHERS. Ciao!

SCAPINO. Oh, Ciao! (Exit SYLVESTRO, GIACINTA and ZERBINETTA.) Nobody's going to say that I give away secrets . . .

(Enter WAITER 1 from cafe, carrying a large sack.)

SCAPINO. . . . and get away with it. (WAITER, with sack, is picking up paper and putting

it in.   At bench he begins singing a
sentimental Irish song.   He continues on
downstage, where SCAPINO picks up
paper, throws it in sack and joining in
on second round of song, takes the sack.
Song ends.   SCAPINO begins clapping,
audience claps.   WAITER takes em-
barrassed bow, crosses upstage, bows
again, exits cafe.   SCAPINO is now DC
with the sack.   He opens it, looks in
and pulls out sausage.   He puts down
sausage and sack, devising plan.)

(GERONTE enters R and crosses downstage toward
    SCAPINO.)

GERONTE.   Well, Scapino, how are you getting on
    with saving my son?
SCAPINO.   Your son, your son, is now
    perfectly safe.   But it's you who now run
    the risk.   You're in the greatest danger,
    sir.   What I wouldn't do to see you locked
    up safely back home.
GERONTE.   Why?
SCAPINO.   Why, at this very moment, sir,
    they're searching everywhere to murder
    you.
GERONTE.   Me?
SCAPINO.   Yes.
GERONTE.   Who?
SCAPINO.   The brother of the girl Ottavio married.
    He thinks that your plan to put your daughter in
    the marriage bed reserved for his sister will
    succeed.   Thinking this, he's determined to wreak
    vengeance on you and make you pay with your life
    for the slight on his family's honor.   At this
    moment all his friends, bullies like himself, they

are questioning every person in this town. I
myself saw a squad of soldiers, all friends of
his, beating up and questioning people, and
laying siege to every way back to your house
so that you can't get home or take a step to right
or left without falling into their hands.

GERONTE. My dear Scapino, what shall I do?

SCAPINO. Well, I don't know, sir, do I? It's a
funny situation. I'm so frightened for you I'm
trembling from hand to mouth. (He pretends to
go and look up every alley, then claps his hands.)
Sir, I have it. I have a way to rescue you. But
first you must get into that sack.

GERONTE. Oh, noooo.

SCAPINO. Ah! Oh, my God, look over there!

GERONTE (jumping into sack, in fear). Who is it?

SCAPINO. Good, good, now you there, all you have to
do is get to the bottom of that sack. Don't make a
sound. Don't make a move. I can then lift you
up, you see, as if you were a bundle. Put you on
my back, carry you through your enemies back to
your house where we can then barricade ourselves
in and then phone for the police.

GERONTE (getting down in sack). A brilliant idea.

SCAPINO (helping him). None better, sir. That's it.
In you go, sir, all the way to the bottom, sir,
and do not make a sound whatever happens.

GERONTE. Just leave it to me. I'll not even breathe.

SCAPINO. Good, good, all the way to the bottom, sir.
That's it. (GERONTE is now in sack. However,
his umbrella is sticking out. SCAPINO pushes it
in, sticking GERONTE who yells.) . . . Just in
time, sir, just in time. Here's a real villainous-
looking one. . . . Now do not make a sound
whatever happens. . . . He's a . . . he's just
sailing up in a boat. (Takes sausage, runs into
boat and picks up broom, fixes hat as a pirate,

jumps out of boat using broom as a crutch, starts
walking to the sack with parrot *[imaginary]* on
shoulder, and takes on assumed voice.)

SCAPINO (as LONG JOHN SILVER). Ah ha! Sixteen men
on a dead man's chest. Yo ho ho and a bottle of
gin. Avast there, ye landlubbers — can any man
Jack of you tell me, Long John Silver, where I
can find that pirate, Geronte. ("Pretty Polly.")
Shut up, you. You over there, you with the sack,
it's Jim lad, isn't it? You tell me where I can
find this Geronte, Jim, and I'll give ye a gold
balloon — I'll give ye a gold doubloon.

SCAPINO (as himself). Sir, sir, are you searching
for my very good friend, Signor Geronte?

SCAPINO (as LONG JOHN SILVER). Ay, that I am,
lad, so that I can keel, haul him, hang him from
the highest yardarm, peck him to death with my
parrot. ("Pretty Polly.") Shut up, you, or I'll
stuff you.

SCAPINO. Sir, I do not know where Signor Geronte is.

SCAPINO (as LONG JOHN SILVER). Jim, lad, you
don't happen to be a shipmate of his, do ye?

SCAPINO. Yes, sir, yes, sir. "I do ye." A very
devoted shipmate.

SCAPINO (as LONG JOHN SILVER). Right then,
Jim — then you take this to him from me --
("Pretty Polly.") -- and her, too. (Attacks the
sack, shouting, etc., as if he were being beaten.)
Ar, you let that be a lesson to you, Jim. Tell
this Geronte that when I find him he'll be my little
bit of treasure, and you know what a pirate does
with a little bit of treasure? ("He buries it.")
He buries it. Right. So now I'm off. Up sail,
up anchor. Up, up and away in my beautiful
doubloon . . . up into the sky . . . (SCAPINO
lies down and begins screaming.)

SCAPINO. Sir, ooh, damn the bully, may they take

his guts for garters.

GERONTE (thrusting his head out of the sack). Oh,
   Scapino, I can't bear it any longer.

SCAPINO. Sir, my back is broken.

GERONTE. How's that? It was my back that he beat.

SCAPINO. Oh, no, no, it wasn't. That was my back
   he was having a go at.

GERONTE. What do you mean? I felt every single
   stroke and I can feel every one of 'em still.

SCAPINO. No, that was only the end of his . . . er,
   yardarm that was reaching you.

GERONTE. You should have moved off a bit then, and
   none of it would have reached me.

SCAPINO. Aagh! (Making GERONTE go back into
   the sack again.) Don't look now, sir, get back
   in as quick as you can. Just spotted another one.
   (Repeat same umbrella business.) Just in time,
   just in time. It's a real vicious Eastern type.
   Not a sound! Not a move, sir! (Long "spiel"
   in stage Japanese a la Karate.) Pardon?
   If you think I'm going to repeat all that,
   you're a stupid idiot. Moment please, there
   is something moving in the saki. I think I am
   going to give gigantic Karate chop suey to
   saki. No, sir, please don't. Sir, that will be
   over my dead body. If necessary. Please
   don't, sir. I've already been beaten up once
   this morning already. Then this is not your
   lucky day! Con foo . . . Ow! . . . Ah so,
   etc. (Short "spiel" and he hits sack again,
   screaming in mock Karate.) You, let that be
   a lesson to you, sonny Jim . . . Teach you not
   to be so insolent. Now I go, Chow . . . Mein.
   Oooh, may they take his guts for garters. (Falls
   on floor.)

GERONTE (popping his head out of the sack). Oh, I'm
   beaten to death.

SCAPINO. Oh, I'm killed.

GERONTE. Why the devil must they keep hitting the
sack?

SCAPINO. I don't know, sir. I mean . . . the ushers
just let them down the aisle. Sir, don't look
'round. I've just spotted another, sir. Get in as
quick as you can. That's it, all the way to the
bottom, and do not make a sound, whatever
happens. (He goes to do umbrella business again
but this time GERONTE pulls it in first.) Just
in time, sir, just in time. It's a whole squad
of English soldiers. (Asks audience to get ready
to march.)

SCAPINO (as SQUAD). I say, sergeant . . . <u>Yes, sir!</u>
. . . I say, sergeant, have you seen that chappie
Geronte anywhere? Hey what, what, what, what.
<u>No, sir! He's not over here.</u> Sir, I say, there's
his servant laddie over there with a sack. Let's
investigate. (To audience.) <u>Company by the</u>
<u>left.</u> Quick. (Audience starts feet, making
marching sounds.) <u>Wait for it</u> . . . (Hits someone on head who has started sound.) <u>By the left,</u>
<u>march, left, right, left, right, left</u> . . . (To
audience.) <u>Keep up in the back there. Left . . .</u>
<u>right . . . left . . . right, left. Brass bands</u>
<u>. . . forward.</u> (Puts sausage to lips, imitates
brass band marching and playing theme from
"The Bridge on the River Kwai.") Then, I say
there, chappie, can you tell us where we can find
Signor Geronte; hey, what, what, what, what,
tallyho what.

SCAPINO. Sir, look, I swear I do not know where he
is. You're the third lot of people that have looked
for him today.

SCAPINO (as SQUAD). Now, look, chappie, either you
tell us where he is or we shall attack your sack.
(Sack falls over; GERONTE has fainted.)

SCAPINO. Sir, sir, for the last time, sir, I do not
    know where he is.
SCAPINO (as SQUAD). Right, then. Sergeant, bring
    up the cavalry. Right! Cavalry -- Forward.
    (Imitates cavalry; stomping and neighing of
    horses.) I say, sergeant! Yes, sir? Keep
    those damn horses quiet. (Then orders.)
    Horses — Quiet! Now for the last time, are
    you going to tell us where we can find Signor
    Geronte?
SCAPINO. Sir, look, for the last time, I swear I
    don't know.
SCAPINO (as SQUAD). Right then, sergeant, prepare
    to charge. (GERONTE pokes head out of sack
    and sees SCAPINO acting as SQUAD.) <u>Yes, sir!</u>
    Artillery, brass band, platoon, my lords, ladies
    and gentlemen, prepare to charge . . . Charge!
    (Just as he is going to turn around and beat the
    sack, he sees GERONTE, who has come out of
    the sack. They stare at each other, then SCAPINO
    runs off, out the upstage exit. GERONTE can't
    catch him because the sack is around his legs.)
GERONTE. The traitor. The villain. The scoundrel.
    (He kicks sack and strains his leg and back.)
    I'll make you pay for this.

(Enter ZERBINETTA down stage R aisle.)

ZERBINETTA (laughing, not seeing GERONTE). Oh,
    I'll die of laughing. Ha, ha, ha, ha. It's too
    funny. (Sits. Laughs.) What a fool the old
    fellow was. (Laughs.)
GERONTE. It's not funny. You've no business to
    laugh at it.
ZERBINETTA. What did you say, signor?
GERONTE. I said you've no right to make fun of me.
ZERBINETTA. Of you?

GERONTE. Yes.

ZERBINETTA. Why, who intends to make fun of you?

GERONTE. You come here to laugh at me to my
    face?

ZERBINETTA. It's nothing to do with you, I was
    laughing to myself at a story I've just heard. The
    funniest ever. (Laughs.) It's about a trick . . .
    (Crosses to and sits in upstage right chair at
    table R.) . . . that was played by a son on his
    father to cheat him of his money.

GERONTE. By a son on his father to cheat him of
    his money?

ZERBINETTA. Yes. And you wouldn't have to press
    me very hard for me to tell you the whole story.
    I'm bursting to tell it to someone.

GERONTE. Then let me press you; tell me it.

ZERBINETTA (slamming GERONTE into chair). Oh,
    thank you. I'll be delighted . . . (She prods him.)
    . . . My young man is in the condition of many a
    suitor. . . . Money is the least of his attributes.
    He has a father who, though he is rich, is the
    meanest of misers. Now what was his name?
    Um . . . (She prods him.) . . . perhaps you can
    help me. Think of someone in this city who is
    known as the greediest, meanest, nastiest of
    all . . .

GERONTE. I wouldn't know him.

ZERBINETTA. There is an "onte" in his name.

GERONTE. "Onte."

ZERBINETTA. "Orante."

GERONTE. "Oronte."

ZERBINETTA. "Organte."

GERONTE. "Argante."

ZERBINETTA. No, no, no . . . Ber . . . Beronte.

GERONTE. Emily Bronte?

ZERBINETTA. Geronte! (She hits him.) That's the
    one. That's the name. He's the meanest man in

Naples! (She hits him. GERONTE crosses and
sits on bench.) The gypsies had decided to leave
town today and my young man was going to lose
me for want of money when he was relieved by
the genius of his servant who got it out of the
miser. As for the servant's name, I'll never
forget it -- it is Scapino.

GERONTE (aside). Hah! The sniveling cockroach.

ZERBINETTA. This is how he tricked . . . (Takes
his umbrella.) . . . the old fool. Ha, ha.
Ha, ha. The thought of it has started me off
again. Ha, ha, ha.

GERONTE. Go on, go on.

ZERBINETTA. He seeks out this Geronte, ha, ha,
ha, and tells him that walking on the quayside
with the son, they were invited aboard a boat
by a friendly Turk. Ha, ha, ha.

GERONTE. I hate Turks.

ZERBINETTA. Ha, ha. Whilst they were eating and
drinking, the boat put to sea, and the Turk sent
poor Scapino by skiff to tell the old miser that
his son would be carried off to Algiers if he did
not pay an immediate ransom of five hundred
thousand lire. The old man just couldn't bring
himself to pay the money, so he tried a hundred
ridiculous ways of getting out of it. After many
windings and turnings, sighs and groans, "What
the devil was he doing on board that boat." Ha,
ha, ha, ha. But as I said, in the end our Scapino
triumphed . . . but you're not laughing. Don't
you think it's funny?

GERONTE (taking back umbrella). The young man's
a scoundrel, an insolent blockhead, and he shall
be punished by his father for the trick he's played.
The gypsy is an inconsiderate, impertinent hussy
to laugh at a man of honor. I'll teach her to come
here debauching people's children. And the valet

is a <u>villain</u> who'll be sent to <u>prison</u> before
<u>tomorrow</u> morning. <u>I hate gypsies.</u> (He exits L.)

(SYLVESTRO enters from cafe.)

SYLVESTRO. Hey . . . did you realize that the old
    fellow you were talking to is your young man's
    father?
ZERBINETTA. I was just beginning to have my
    suspicions; I told him his own story before I
    realized it.
SYLVESTRO. What, his own story?
ZERBINETTA. Yes. I was bursting to tell it to
    someone. Oh . . . (An Italian expletive.) . . .
    what does it matter? Things can't get any worse
    for us.
SYLVESTRO. Your tongue must be long enough for
    two. You can't even keep your own secrets.
ZERBINETTA. Oh, yaaaahhh! (Sticks tongue out
    at him.)

(ARGANTE enters from stage R aisle.)

ARGANTE (off). Hey there, Sylvestro.
SYLVESTRO. Get inside. There's my master calling
    me. (ZERBINETTA exits into cafe.)
ARGANTE (coming to bench). So, you and that other
    rascal Scapino have conspired together to cheat
    me, and my son's in it, too. Do you think I'm
    going to stand for it?
SYLVESTRO. Yes!
BOTH. No!

(GERONTE enters from UC.)

SYLVESTRO. Now, really, sir. If that scoundrel,
    Scapino, has played you some trick or other, I

wash my hands of the whole affair.

ARGANTE.   I'm not going to let myself be made a
fool of.

SYLVESTRO.   Yes . . . er . . . No! (Exits to cafe.
(GERONTE sits on end of bench; other end goes
up.)

GERONTE.   Ah, Signor Argante, you see me weighed
down by misfortune. (ARGANTE sits on other
end, and bench levels.)

ARGANTE.   You see me, too, Signor Geronte, in the
slough of despond.

GERONTE.   That criminal Scapino has tricked me
out of five hundred thousand lire.

ARGANTE.   And that self-same criminal Scapino has
cheated me, too, of two hundred thousand lire.

GERONTE.   Not only did he trick me out of five
hundred thousand lire, he's treated me in a way
which I'm too ashamed to explain! But I'll pay
him back for it.

ARGANTE.   I'll make sure he pays for the tricks he's
played on us.

(SYLVESTRO has appeared on the cafe balcony.)

SYLVESTRO (aside).   Please, God, don't let them
find out I was mixed up in all this.

GERONTE.   But this isn't the end of the story, Signor
Argante. One misfortune follows another . . .
the daughter I expected to arrive today is lost.
She and her mother set out some time ago from
Marseilles and are reported to have been lost in
the ship they sailed in.

(NURSE enters from cafe, crosses R.)

ARGANTE.   Why, oh, why, did you not bring her
here with you?

GERONTE. Reasons, reasons! Business and family
     interests forced me to keep this second marriage
     a great secret.

NURSE. Oh, Signor Pandolfo!

GERONTE (standing). You here, nurse?

NURSE (falling on her knees). Oh, Signor Pandolfo . . .

GERONTE (opening umbrella to block ARGANTE's
     vision). Don't call me Pandolfo here. Call me
     Geronte. The reasons which forced me to take
     another name at Marseilles exist no longer.

NURSE. Alas, what troubles this change of name
     has caused us in trying to find you here.

GERONTE. Us? Then where are my daughter and
     her mother?

NURSE. Your daughter, signor, is close by. But
     before you see her, I must beg you to forgive us,
     for we were penniless and starving and thought
     we should never see you again. I must beg you
     to forgive me for having let her be married.
     (ARGANTE stands, crosses to them.)

GERONTE. My daughter married?

NURSE. Yes, sir.

GERONTE. To whom?

NURSE. To a young gentleman called Ottavio, son
     of a certain Signor Argante.

GERONTE. Good God!

ARGANTE. What a coincidence!

GERONTE (starting downstage). Show us, show us
     quickly where she is.

NURSE. Follow me into that house over there.
     (NURSE, ARGANTE and GERONTE exit stage
     R aisle.)

SYLVESTRO (on balcony). Well. I'd never believe it
     if I hadn't seen it with my own ears . . .

(SCAPINO enters balcony.)

SCAPINO. Well, Sylvestro, how's tricks?

SYLVESTRO. I've got two little bits of information
for you. One's a surprise. Ottavio's worries
are over. Our Giacinta turns out to be none
other than Signor Geronte's daughter. Luck's
brought about the very thing the fathers most
intended. The other bit of information, no
surprise, is that both the fathers are full of
terrifying threats about your future, especially
Signor Geronte.

SCAPINO. Well, threats never did anyone harm,
did they? They're clouds passing by, high in
the sky. (Spoken like poetry.)

SYLVESTRO. Yes, well, just you watch out. I
wouldn't put it past those two boys to make it
up with their fathers, and then where would you
be, eh?

SCAPINO. Yes, well, just you leave that to me.

SYLVESTRO. Hey, hide yourself. Here they come.
(SCAPINO exits.)

(Enter GERONTE, ARGANTE, NURSE and GIACINTA
down stage R aisle.)

GERONTE. Come along, my dear. Come home with
me. My happiness would have been complete if
only I'd been able to see your mother with you.

ARGANTE. Here comes Ottavio, right on cue.

(OTTAVIO enters from cafe. SYLVESTRO exits
balcony.)

ARGANTE. Come, son, come celebrate with us the
happy occasion of your marriage.

OTTAVIO (who has not seen GIACINTA). No, Father,
all your plans of marriage mean nothing to me.
I must be plain with you; you have heard of the

secret marriage I made.
ARGANTE. Yes, but you don't know . . .

(SYLVESTRO enters from cafe.)

OTTAVIO. I know all I need to know.
ARGANTE. I must tell you about Signor Geronte's
    daughter.
OTTAVIO. Signor Geronte's daughter means nothing
    to me.
GERONTE. But she's the one . . .
OTTAVIO. No, sir, I will not be shaken.
SYLVESTRO. Just let him get a . . .
OTTAVIO. Shut up, you. I don't want to hear.
ARGANTE. Your wife . . .
OTTAVIO. No, Father, I'll die rather than desert
    my lovely Giacinta. (Crossing to her.) This is
    the girl to whom I'm married; I'll love her all my
    life and never even look at another woman.
ARGANTE. But she's the one we want you to have.
    Oh, my God. What an idiot he is. Never listens
    to anyone but himself.

(Enter ZERBINETTA from cafe.)

GIACINTA. It's true, Ottavio. This is the father I
    have lost. All our troubles are over. Zerbinetta!
    (Going to her.) Father, please don't let me be
    separated from this dear friend; if you knew her,
    you would love her as much as I do. (All move
    upstage.)
GERONTE. You want me to allow a creature who's
    ensnared your brother into my house, a creature
    who threw a thousand insults in my face not half
    an hour ago?
ZERBINETTA. Sir, forgive me. I should never have
    spoken in that way if I'd known it was you, and

then I only knew you by repute.

GERONTE. What do you mean, "repute"?

ZERBINETTA. As the meanest, most greediest . . .
   (GERONTE goes for her. She moves away.)

GIACINTA. Father, my brother's love for her is
   deep and true, and I'll answer for her virtue.
   (OTTAVIO moves to her.)

GERONTE. That's all very well. Would you have
   me marry my son to her? A girl of the streets,
   that nobody knows?

(LEANDRO enters stage L house aisle.)

LEANDRO. Father!

GERONTE. Yes.

LEANDRO. You need no longer complain that I love
   a girl without a name or fortune. The gypsies
   who sold her to me revealed she was born in
   this city . . .

OTHERS. City?

LEANDRO. And to a well-known family . . .

OTHERS. Family!

LEANDRO. They stole her away when she was four
   years old.

OTHERS. Four!

LEANDRO (going to ZERBINETTA). And here is a
   bracelet that may reveal to us . . . that may
   reveal to us exactly who her real parents are.
   (Takes off her bracelet; holds it in air.)

ARGANTE (reaching over, taking bracelet with cane).
   Unbelievable! This bracelet proves she's my very
   own daughter whom I lost at the age you spoke of.

GERONTE. Your daughter?

ARGANTE. Yes, indeed. And now I look closely I
   see in her face all our family features.

ZERBINETTA. Father! (She embraces ARGANTE.)

GIACINTA. Goodness me, what an extraordinary

coincidence!

(CARLO enters. All begin to move upstage as
     HEADWAITER and WAITER 2 bring table from
     cafe and set it at UC and LEANDRO and OTTAVIO
     position bench in front of table.)

CARLO. Signores, there has been a terrible accidente.
ALL. Accidente?
CARLO. Poor Scapino!
ALL. Scapino?
GERONTE. I will see that wretch hanged.
CARLO. Oh, sir, you won't have to worry yourself
     about that. As he was passing by the scaffolding
     of a new building a stone-cutter's hammer fell
     on his head. . . .

(WAITER 1 starts down stage L aisle carrying SCAPINO
     over his shoulder.)

ALL. Oh!
CARLO.   . . . fractured his skull . . .
ALL. Oh!
CARLO.   . . . and scattered his brains up . . .
     (Points.) . . . and down . . . (Points.) . . . the
     street.
ALL. Ugh!
CARLO. He's dying and his last wish is to be brought
     here to say a few last words to you all.
ARGANTE. Where is he?
CARLO. Here he comes now.

(Enter SCAPINO carried by WAITER 1. His head is
     bandaged.)

ALL. Oh! . . . (SCAPINO moans.) Oh! . . .
     (SCAPINO moans.) Oh! . . . (WAITER places

him on table UC.)

SCAPINO (groaning). Ooooh, oooh. Signores,
    signores, you see me now . . . you see me in this
    tragic state. (Moans.)

ALL. Oh.

SCAPINO. Signores . . . Before I die I had to come
    to beg forgiveness of all those that I've ever
    offended. (Moans.)

ALL. Ooooh!

SCAPINO. Yes, signores, before I breathe my last
    breath I beg you from the bottom of your hearts
    to forgive me everything I've ever done. . . .

ALL. Si, si . . .

SCAPINO. . . . especially Signor Argante and
    Signor Geronte . . .

ARGANTE. For my part, Scapino, I forgive you.

ALL. Bravo.

ARGANTE. Go and die in peace.

SCAPINO (to GERONTE). But it's you, Signor Geronte,
    that I have offended most with that cruel beating
    I gave you earlier . . .

GERONTE. Don't exhaust yourself. I forgive you as
    well.

SCAPINO. But it was a horrible cheek of me to give
    you that good hiding in the sack . . .

ALL. Hiding . . . sack . . . etc.

GERONTE. Let's forget it.

SCAPINO. Now that I am dying, sir, I can't express
    my sorrow enough for that sausage trick I played
    on . . .

ALL. Sausage?

GERONTE. Oh, God, shut up!

SCAPINO. The sausage trick when he was in the
    sack . . .

GERONTE. Shut up. I tell you. I've forgiven you
    everything.

SCAPINO. Oh, what joy, sir. Do you really forgive

me from the bottom of your heart the uh . . .
pretty polly . . . (ALL laugh.)

GERONTE. Yes, yes, yes, I forgive you everything.

SCAPINO. Sir, I can't tell you how much better I
feel for those few kind words.

GERONTE. Quite. But I forgive you only on one
condition.

SCAPINO. What?

GERONTE. That you die. If you recover, I take it
all back.

ALL. Oooooh!

SCAPINO (more groans). Ooooh, oooh, sir, I'm
sinking fast . . . I'm feeling weaker every
moment.

ARGANTE. Signor Geronte, to celebrate our
happiness, I beg you to forgive him unconditionally.

ALL (running to audience). Si, si . . . Forgive him,
forgive . . . forgive him. . . .

GERONTE (screaming). Basta! Basta! (To ACTORS
and audience.) Shall I forgive him?

ALL. Yes!

GERONTE.   . . . No!

ALL. Yes!

GERONTE.   . . . No!

ALL. Yes! (GERONTE raises his hand. There is
silence.)

GERONTE. All right, I forgive him.

ALL. Hooray! (Shouts and applause. EVERYONE
runs for glasses, sings and dances fast version of
"Minestrone Macaroni.")

> Pollo All Americana,
> Scampi Fritti In Bordo
> Vermichelli
> Talliachelli
> Capuchino Espresso.

Minestrone Macaroni,
Ravioli Aux Crevette,
Caramella In Padella,
Avocado Vinaigrette.

Scallopina Valdostana,
Bistecca Con Risotto,
Vermichelli
Talliachelli
Da Un Buon Appetito.

Minestrone Macaroni
Ravioli Aux Crevette
Caramella In Padella
Avocado Vinaigrette.
(Once through; then repeat first two verses;
toast, drink and throw glasses. At end of song
they throw plastic glasses to audience and do
slow instrumental humming song as they exit
audience aisles. SCAPINO exits last, cafe.)

GROUP curtain call.

SCAPINO curtain call. SCAPINO calls all on
stage. They come out and sit. WAITER 2 brings
SCAPINO his guitar. SCAPINO talks to audience.

SCAPINO. Ladies and gentlemen . . . wait a
minute . . . we're not finished yet. I'll tell
you why -- we're not going home yet because
there is one song in this show that we have been
singing from the word go. It goes like this.
(Hums "Minestrone Macaroni" melody.) We
were singing it at the very end. Now as I was
looking out, all of you were smiling . . . all of
you . . . and then we got to the musical instruments and all of it changed . . . it changed to

"what a bunch of idiots, " so tonight we are going
to split the audience right down the center . . .
so . . . you, sir . . . you . . . he's grinning
away . . . cross your legs or move to the right
. . . we will have . . . (To CAST.) . . . what
do you want . . . (Trombones, mandolins.)
. . . right . . . (To audience.) . . . this side
trombones, this mandolins . . . no, really, you
can get the most romantic sound . . . all you
have to do is make sure you spit directly on the
neck of the person in front of you . . . right
then . . . in the back . . . (Pointing to GERONTE,
ARGANTE, NURSE.) . . . the old dears, the
cellos . . . (NURSE spreads her legs.
Laughs. SCAPINO turns to her.) . . . put it
down . . . right, then . . . this side trombones
. . . this side mandolins . . . all the adults be
kids again . . . it's a marvelous feeling, I promise
you . . . (Starts to play.) . . . Wait a minute
. . . ladies and gentlemen, I would like to bring
to your attention that in our audience tonight
there are three people who are not enjoying
themselves one bit . . . I mean it. There are
three people among you who are hating every
minute of this . . . we got little peepholes in
the set and we watch you all night long . . . now
those three people wherever you are, we know
exactly where you are sitting . . . that's all
right, though, we know some people don't like
clowning about . . . that's all right . . . you sit
back and relax, we'll make idiots of ourselves
. . . then we'll stop . . . point to you . . . and
you'll stand up and do it on your own . . . right,
then . . . here we go.

ALL mime instruments and hum together as
CAST goes among audience and then exits.

Final curtain calls.

Then WAITRESS comes out and kicks jukebox
for the last time and it plays.

END OF PLAY

PRODUCTION NOTES

THE SETTING:
The Italian commedia at its most basic needed
nothing more than a couple of boards raised on
trestles, with perhaps a blanket thrown over some
poles to form a backdrop. A true son of its ancient
father, SCAPINO can also get along with the bare
essentials -- the simpler the better. Not that anyone has to stage SCAPINO with splintery old boards,
sawhorses, and a moldy blanket. Not at all!
SCAPINO can and should be visual fun for the
audience's eyes. But it doesn't have to be
complicated.
The setting of the play is a dockside cafe in
Naples, and the main elements on stage are the
cafe with its balconies L and R, sidewalk, ramps
and a jetty (the forestage). Upstage of the jetty is
a bit of the (imaginary) sea, where the boat is
located. The sea, of course, is the Bay of Naples.
The stage chart shown here (page 90) is of the
set designed by Carl Toms for the Broadway production.
However, this is offered only as a starting point for
your imagination; if you can think of something differ-
ent, easier or better, don't be afraid to try. The
main thing about the set is that it shouldn't be too
pretty or too decorative. The important thing is the
feeling of the Mediterranean, blue skies and hot sun.
Any attempt at scene-painting should be avoided,
especially if the people involved are not very adept
at it. It would be better to indicate the Mediterranean
sky with a large blue flat and the sun with a large
yellow one. The water on stage is not real -- it is
represented by a blue ground-cloth. The boat is
real, however, as are the gaudy decorations. These

touches of reality can convince the audience of the basic intense reality of the play, even though some parts of the action may be almost unreal.

PROPERTIES:
GENERAL PROPERTIES:
Three round tables (one with umbrella), each with two or three chairs; jukebox with records, bench, small rowboat, coil of rope, garbage can, broom (with rubber crutch tip on handle) in boat; rope hanging down left side of balcony R; large barrel. Assorted crates, barrels, boxes, baskets, cans, etc. Optional decorations: posters, strings of onion or garlic, Chianti bottles, colored lights, clotheslines with clothes, netting, etc. as desired to dress the stage. When the play opens, there are three tablecloths hung over the balcony railing at L.

PERSONAL PROPERTIES:
Part One
WAITRESS: Five coins, checked tablecloth, wine carafe and glasses.
CARLO: Bicycle, bottle opener, glass of Coke, bottle of Coke; shoeshine kit with rag, brush, polish; old-fashioned telephone (without cord).
WAITER 1: Broom, handlebars of bicycle; napkin with spoon and fork; plate of spaghetti.
WAITER 2: Broom, bicycle wheel, bicycle seat; rolls in basket.
HEADWAITER: Menu, order pad and pencil, bill on plate, coin, napkin.
SCAPINO: Guitar, sausage (artificial).
SYLVESTRO: Chocolate bar in pocket, two bottles of Coke and two glasses, money, bicycle chain.
ARGANTE: Cane, wallet containing money.

GERONTE: Umbrella, key, money in wallet.
LEANDRO: Sunglasses.

Intermission
WAITRESS: Five coins, hero sandwich.

Part Two
NURSE: Handkerchief in handbag.
HEADWAITER: Piece of chalk.
WAITER 1: Large sack containing sausage (artificial).
CARLO: Ice cream box with neck strap (cones, ice
    cream balls and dixie cup of ice cream), ice
    cream scoop.
SCAPINO: Guitar; bandage on head (end of play).
LEANDRO: Bottle of chianti.
ZERBINETTA. Bracelet.

Note: If any spaghetti or Coke is spilled on the stage,
    it must be swept or mopped up as soon as possible,
    in order to prevent accidents. Also, the fork and
    knife must not be so loosely wrapped that they
    might slip out of the napkin during the throwing.

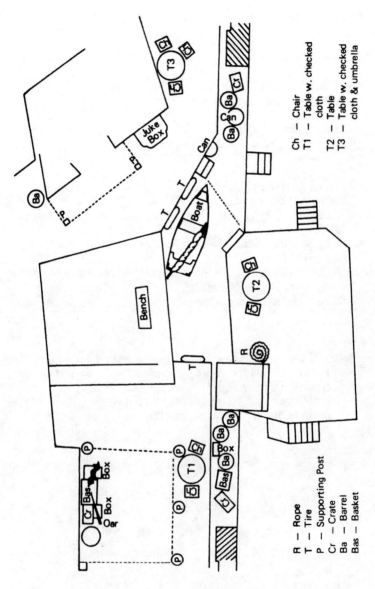

Ch — Chair
T1 — Table w. checked cloth
T2 — Table
T3 — Table w. checked cloth & umbrella

R — Rope
T — Tire
P — Supporting Post
Cr — Crate
Ba — Barrel
Bas — Basket

90

MINESTRONI MACARONI
(slow version)

Words and Music by
FRANK DUNLOP and JIM DALE

(Introduction)

Pol-lo All A-mer-i- ca-na,   Scam-pi Frit-ti in Bro-do,
Scal-lo pi-na Val-do-sta-na,   Bis-tec-ca con Ris-so-to,

Pas-ta Bo-lo-gne - se Pa-te May-on - nai-se, Ca-pu-chi-no Es-pres-so.
Pas-ta Bo-lo-gne - se Pa-te May-on - nai-se, Da Un Buon Ap-pe- ti -to.

Mi-ne - stro-ni Ma-ca - ro-ni, Ra-vi - o - li Aux Cre-vet-te, Cara-

mel-la In Pa - del-la, A-vo - ca-do Vi - nai-gret-te.   gret-te.

MINESTRONI MACARONI
(Fast version)

Words and Music By
Jim Dale and Frank Dunlop

CHOW CHOW FOR NOW

Words and Music
Jim Dale and Frank Dunlop

Oh So - le mi - o, Chow Chow bam- bi- no, Three pounds per ki - lo, ser - ra, ser - ra. Ri - bi- na, Frank Dun-lo- pil-lo, A - jax et Bril-lo and To - ny Quinn. La Dol-che vi - ta, So - phi - a Pon - te, Moon-light in Ver-mon - te, ser-ra ser - ra. Chin - za-no et Mi - a Far-row, Un - til to - mor-row, chow chow for now. O - le.